Daily
Reflection

Daily
Reflection

Selected by
Diane Allen

PADRE PIO
PRESS

Other Books by Diane Allen

Pray, Hope, and Don't Worry: True Stories of Padre Pio

Pray, Hope, and Don't Worry: True Stories of Padre Pio Book II

Published by Padre Pio Press
Post Office Box 191545
San Diego, CA 92159

ISBN 0983710562
ISBN 13 97809837105-6-1

Introduction

From the time I was a teenager, I have loved spiritual reading. I have made it a habit to keep a little book of spiritual reflections close by and I refer to them daily. I need the inspiration and the guidance I receive from such reading so that I can keep my heart open and receptive to the presence of God. When I lose my perspective and my peace of mind, I turn to the saints, and to other holy men and women of God. Their wisdom is like a shining lamp that illuminates my path, leading me back to the right course.

I have carefully selected the meditations that are in this book and have gathered them over a period of many years. The healing thoughts and prayers contained in this volume are meant to enlighten, inspire, and uplift the soul.

- Diane Allen

Your word is very pure Lord,
and your servant loves it.

- Psalm 119:14

The Blessed Virgin is the Queen of heaven and earth, quite true, but she is more Mother than Queen.

- St. Therese of Lisieux

L et us visit Christ wherever we may be. Let us care for him, feed him, clothe him, welcome him, honor him - not only at a meal, as some have done, or by anointing him, as Mary did, not only by lending him a tomb, like Joseph of Arimathea did, or by arranging for his burial, like Nicodemus, not only by giving him gold, frankincense and myrrh, like the Magi did before all the others. The Lord of all asks for mercy and sacrifice, and mercy is greater . . . Let us then show him mercy in the persons of the poor and those who today are lying on the ground, so that when we come to leave this world, we may be received into an everlasting dwelling place, by Christ our Lord. Amen

- St. Gregory of Nazianzen

O Jesus, I see this new year as a blank page that your Father is giving me, upon which he will write day by day what he has arranged for me in his divine pleasure. With full confidence I am writing at the top of the page from now on, "Lord, do with me what you will." And at the bottom I have already put my "amen" to every disposition of your divine will. Yes, O Lord, I say "yes" to all the joys, to all the sorrows, to all the graces, to all the hardships that you have prepared for me and which you will be revealing to me day by day. Let my "amen" be the Paschal amen, always followed by alleluia, uttered with all my heart.

- Sister Carmela of the Holy Ghost

Everything that Christ said and did and experienced on earth is the Word saying, "See how God loves you!". . . Looking at the world today, it is not easy to believe that everywhere Christ is born again, that God looks down on the wreckage and misery - the fiasco, if you like - that we have made of this world, and seeing us in the midst of it says, *This is my well beloved Son.* But this is so, and however difficult or however insignificant our life may seem to be, it is precious to God as Christ is precious to God. On each one in whom Christ lives, the whole of the infinite love of God is concentrated at every moment . . . If it were not for Christ in us, we would not be able to trust. We are too weak; we could not believe in God's goodness if we had only ourselves to believe with; neither could we love one another if we had only ourselves to love with. We can trust God with Christ's trust in the Father; that is the trust which is our rest.

- Caryll Houselander

Precisely because our secular milieu offers us so few spiritual disciplines, we have to develop our own. We have, indeed, to fashion our own desert where we can withdraw every day, shake off our compulsions, and dwell in the gentle healing presence of our Lord. Without such a desert we will lose our own soul while preaching the gospel to others, but with such a spiritual abode, we will become increasingly conformed to him in whose name we minister . . . Solitude is its own end. It is the place where Christ remodels us in his own image and frees us from the victimizing compulsions of the world. Solitude is the place of our salvation.

- Henri Nouwen

Each of you has but one thing to do, become a companion to Jesus, a companion and a friend - a friend who, once and for all, consents to shoulder the same love, with eyes turned with his to the Cross as the sole source of the world's salvation . . . It is thus that Jesus means to teach you to live like him. Like him, you will see that the will of the Father is that you shall work for the salvation of your fellow men . . . with the giving of the whole of your lives, with the immolation of your egoism, with open and unreserved friendship for every human being.

- Father Rene Voillaume

What is needed today is for the Christian to encounter God in his everyday life. Jesus can no longer be a distant stranger, respected and feared - or even loved - but uninvolved in life . . . Man knows that he is only a creature and a weak and vulnerable creature at that; but he knows too that he has been offered the opportunity to become a son of God and a collaborator in the kingdom that is being founded. He knows that he must diminish so that God may increase . . . The Holy Spirit is telling us that life today, like life yesterday, is not a "punishment." It is a gift of love from the Creator. It is not an obstacle to divine union; it is the customary place for a meeting with Christ.

- Father Michel Quoist

Death and eternity are the two faces of one great destiny. Nothing is in vain; nothing dies. Our life on earth is completed, crowned, and perpetuated in heaven. Earthly life is beautiful and worthy when it is lived in the service of God. All that is beautiful and good in us and around us on earth and in the universe is a mere pallid image of the kingdom of God. The higher one rises toward heaven, the more he understands the great mystery of life which has as its aim: goodness, happiness, God.

- Giorgio Berlutti

We shall have no enemies in heaven. We shall never lose a friend. God's praises are sung both there and here, but here they are sung in anxiety, there, in security; here they are sung by those destined to die, there, by those destined to live forever . . . here they are sung by wayfarers, there, by those living in their own country. So then, my brothers, let us sing now, not in order to enjoy a life of leisure, but in order to lighten our labors. You should sing as wayfarers do; sing, but continue your journey. Do not be lazy, but sing to make your journey more enjoyable. Sing, but keep going. What do I mean by keep going? Keep on making progress. This progress, however, must be in virtue; for there are some, the Apostle warns, whose only progress is in vice . . . Sing then, but keep going.

- St. Augustine

If you love truth, be a lover of silence. Silence, like the sunlight, will illuminate you in God and will deliver you from the phantoms of ignorance. Silence will unite you to God . . . More than all things, love silence. It is fruitful in a way that words cannot describe. In the beginning we have to force ourselves to be silent. But then there is born something that draws us to silence. May God give you an experience of this "something" that is born of silence.

- Isaac of Niniveh

Remember that you have only one soul; that you have only one death to die; that you have only one life, which is short and has to be lived by you alone; and that there is only one glory, which is eternal. If you do this, there will be many things about which you care nothing.

- St. Teresa of Avila

When Jesus wanted to speak about the life of the Spirit in us, he used the figure of a gushing spring. It is like living water that must become in us, a spring that wells up to eternal life (John 4:14). Prayer is that deep spring in us. Actually it was there all along as the breath of the Holy Spirit who was actively and unceasingly praying within us. We did not notice it. Without knowing it, we had piled up numerous stones around that spring . . . We must be very careful, for it could well be precisely our efforts that form the stones obstructing the natural gushing of the spring without our knowing it. In order to pray more and better we must often do less, let go of more things, give up numerous good intentions, and be content to yield to the inner pressure of the Spirit the moment he bubbles up in us and tries to win us over and take us in tow.

- Father Andre Louf, O.C.S.O.

Bless me, Jesus, and bless me altogether, my soul, my body, my senses, and my faculties. Bless especially my tongue, that it may only speak for your glory. Bless my eyes, that they may not look at anything that might tempt me to displease you. Bless my taste that it may not offend you by intemperance; and bless all the members of my body, that they may all serve you and not offend you. Bless my memory, that it may always remember your love and the favors you have accorded me. Bless my understanding, that it may know your goodness and the obligation I have of loving you; and that it may see all that I must avoid and all that I must do, to conform myself to your holy will. Above all, bless my will, that it may love no other but you, the infinite good, that it may seek for nothing but to please you and may take delight in nothing but what conduces to your glory.

- St. Alphonsus Liguori

Love of neighbor is thus shown to be possible in the way proclaimed by the Bible, by Jesus. It consists in the very fact that, in God and with God, I love even the person whom I do not like or even know. This can only take place on the basis of an intimate encounter with God, an encounter which has become a communion of will . . . Then I learn to look on this other person not simply with my eyes and my feelings, but from the perspective of Jesus Christ. His friend is my friend . . . Seeing with the eyes of Christ, I can give to others much more than their outward necessities; I can give them the look of love which they crave . . . If I have no contact whatsoever with God in my life, then I cannot see in the other, anything more than the other, and I am incapable of seeing in him the image of God . . . Only my readiness to encounter my neighbor and to show him love makes me sensitive to God as well. Only if I serve my neighbor can my eyes be opened to what God does for me and how much he loves me.

- Pope Benedict XVI

I was hungry, and you gave me to eat: I was thirsty, and you gave me to drink: I was naked and you covered me: I was in prison and you came to me, sick and you visited me. Lord when did we see you hungry, thirsty, sick and we aided thee? As long as you did it to one of these my least brethren, you did it to me. (Matthew 25:35- 40)

Christ, therefore, is present in suffering. It is he who receives our attention, our generosity, our charity, who implores it . . . It will be he who will reward it, and will reward it with a kingdom, not a human, fleeting one, but one prepared by God . . . From this presence of Christ in a brother who suffers, is born for each of us, the duty to bring relief for suffering . . . We cannot offer Christ the crumbs which fall from the table of one who is satiated. The crumbs, in the words of the Gospel, are for the dogs. But when he who hungers is Christ, when the homeless one is Christ, what would we not do for him, and what can ever be worthy of him no matter what we do?

- Cardinal Giacomo Lercaro

Our utter, complete forgetfulness of God the Father is a tragedy . . . Why do we not turn to him at all times? Why don't we pray to him? Run to him? Love and adore him constantly and greatly? Where is our devotion to God the Father? Today more than ever in history, we need him. We are frightened beyond the ordinary fears of humanity, living as we do under the shadow of strange bombs that in the twinkling of an eye can destroy us and the very earth we tread. If only we turned our faces toward him, who loves us as only a Father can . . . Let us fall on our knees and, embracing his feet, implore our Father to forgive us our forgetfulness, our neglect, begging him to take us once more into his arms, and make us safe.

- Catherine De Hueck Doherty

So long as we live in this world we cannot escape suffering and temptation. Whence it is written in Job: *The life of man upon earth is a warfare* (Job 7:1) . . . Yet temptations, though troublesome and severe, are often useful to a man, for in them he is humbled, purified, and instructed. The saints all passed through many temptations and trials to profit by them, while those who could not resist became reprobate and fell away. There is no state so holy, no place so secret, that temptations and trials will not come. Man is never safe from them as long as he lives, for they come from within us . . . Often we do not know what we can stand, but temptation shows us what we are . . . Let us humble our souls under the hand of God in every trial and temptation for he will save and exalt the humble in spirit.

- Thomas à Kempis

It will be of great importance if you can leave aside your cares and spend the remainder of your life only in worshiping God. He requires no great matters of us; a little remembrance of him from time to time; a little adoration; sometimes to pray for his grace, sometimes to offer him your sufferings, and sometimes to return him thanks for the favors he has given you, and still gives you, in the midst of your troubles . . . Lift up your heart to him, sometimes even at your meals, and when you are in company; the least little remembrance will always be acceptable to him. You need not cry very loud; he is nearer to us than we are aware of.

- Brother Lawrence of the Resurrection

We have not deserved to pray; but God, in his goodness, has permitted us to speak to him. Our prayer is an incense which he receives with extreme pleasure. My children, your heart is poor and narrow; but prayer enlarges it, and renders it capable of loving God. Prayer is a foretaste of heaven, an overflow of paradise. It never leaves us without sweetness . . . Troubles melt away before a fervent prayer like snow before the sun.

- St. John Vianney

Lord, lead me to a meditation on life eternal. The fulfillment I seek can never be found amid the fragments of earthly existence . . . I need meditation to keep my passing days in mortal perspective - to hear, in worldly sounds, your voice most pure. Lord, in quiet meditation I wait upon your word. I meet you to whom in silence I shall one day return. Without you, I accomplish nothing. Only when your spirit guides me can I be your faithful servant.

- Susan Muto

Costly grace is the gospel which must be sought again and again and again, the gift which must be asked for, the door at which a man must knock. Such grace is costly because it calls us to follow, and it is grace because it calls us to follow Jesus Christ. It is costly because it costs a man his life, and it is grace because it gives a man the only true life. It is costly because it condemns sin, and grace because it justifies the sinner. Above all, it is costly because it cost God the life of his Son: *You were bought at a price* - and what has cost God much cannot be cheap for us. God did not reckon his Son too dear a price to pay for our life, but delivered him up for us. Costly grace is the Incarnation of God.

- Dietrich Bonhoeffer

F*ather* – with this word I express my certainty that someone is there who hears me, who never leaves me alone, who is always present. I express my certainty that God, despite the infinite difference between him and me, is such that I can speak to him, may even address him familiarly as "thou." His greatness does not overwhelm me . . . I am so important to him, I belong so closely to him, that I can rightly address him as Father. My being born is not a mistake, then, but a grace . . . I am wanted; not a child of chance or necessity, but of choice and freedom. Therefore I shall always have a purpose in life; there will always be a meaning for me, a task designed just for me; there is a conception of me that I can seek and find and fulfill.

- Pope Benedict XVI

We must be ready to carry the burden of anyone whom we meet on our way, and who clearly needs help - not only those who deserve or seem to deserve help. Everyone is our "business" and Christ in everyone, potentially or actually, has a first claim on us, a claim that comes before all else. We are here on earth to help carry the cross of Christ, the Christ hidden in other men, and to help in whatever way we can. We may, like Simon, have literally a strong arm to give; we may help to do hard work, we may have material goods to give; we may have time, which we desperately want for our self, but which we must sacrifice for Christ in man; we may have only suffering . . . We do not look for Christ only in saints; we look for him, perceive him by faith, and try to help him, most of all in sinners. It is in sinners that Christ suffers most today, in them that his need is most urgent.

- Caryll Houselander

The trouble with us is that we want to serve God in our own way and not in his, and according to our own will, not his. When he permits that we be ill, we want to be well; when he wills that we serve him in sufferings, we desire to serve him with works; when he wants us to exercise charity, we want to exercise humility; when he wants resignation from us, we want devotion, piety or some other virtue. And this, not because the things we want are more pleasing to him, but because they give us greater satisfaction. This undoubtedly is the greatest impediment to our perfection, because if we want to become saints according to our will, we will never become saints. In order really to become a saint it is best to do so according to God's will.

- St. Francis de Sales

In the face of God's designs, our attitude will be one of abandonment. To give ourselves to God, to place within his hands our personality, our own views, in order to accept his, such will be the order we follow . . . At present, God hides from me, certain of his designs over me. I ought to find it well that he hides them from me, without troubling myself. I do not know if I shall live a long time, or if I shall die soon, if I shall remain in good health, or if sickness will weigh me down, if I shall keep my faculties, or if I shall lose them. And what am I to do? To lose myself in adoration. To adore God as Principle, as Wisdom, as Justice, as Infinite Goodness. To throw myself in his arms, like a child in the arms of its mother . . . I know that his adorable will plans my holiness. I must surrender myself entirely to his action, with faith, confidence and love.

- Blessed Columba Marmion

On earth we must be attached to nothing, not even to the most innocent things, for they fail you just when you least expect it. Only the things that are eternal can content us.

- St. Therese of Lisieux

To be a child of love, is to sacrifice oneself to the love of God for the conversion of sinners . . . If we had to pray hundreds of years in order to have a man brought back to the love of God, we would have reason enough to rejoice on account of it . . . Ask God that all your actions, from the beginning of your existence, be actions of love for God, performed in union with the sorrowful passion of Jesus.

- Father Paul of Moll, O.S.B.

Lord, Father, all-powerful and ever-living God, I thank you, for even though I am a sinner . . . not because of my worth but in the kindness of your mercy, you have fed me with the precious Body and Blood of your Son, our Lord Jesus Christ. I pray that this Holy Communion may not bring me condemnation . . . but forgiveness and salvation. May it be a helmet of faith and a shield of goodwill. May it purify me from evil ways and put an end to my evil passions. May it bring me charity and patience, humility and obedience, and growth in the power to do good. May it be my strong defense against all my enemies, visible and invisible, and the perfect calming of all my evil impulses, bodily and spiritual. May it unite me more closely to you, the one true God, and lead me safely through death to everlasting happiness with you. And I pray that you will lead me, a sinner, to the banquet where you, with your Son and Holy Spirit are true and perfect light, total fulfillment, everlasting joy, gladness without end, and perfect happiness to your saints. Grant this through Christ our Lord. Amen

- St. Thomas Aquinas

Always ask yourself, "What would the Lord do?" and then do it. This is your one but absolute rule . . . The thing to do is to keep our eyes fixed upon Jesus, asking ourselves, we his Little Brothers, what he would do in our place. The world has little need for us to present it with any new "formula" . . . People are dying of hunger and thirst because they are so far away from him who is Life, and what they want is a presence - the presence of Life. Unknowingly, they are seeking a person, a divine person, and this person is Love Incarnate, Jesus. They will seek him in us.

- Father Rene Voillaume

If we knew how to listen to God, we would hear him speaking to us. For God does speak. He speaks in his Gospels. He also speaks through life - that new gospel to which we ourselves add a page each day. But we are rarely open to God's message, because our faith is too weak and our life too earthbound . . . To have faith is not only to raise one's eyes to God to contemplate him; it is also to look at this world, with Christ's eyes. If we had allowed Christ to penetrate our whole being, if we had purified ourselves, the world would no longer be an obstacle. It would be a perpetual incentive to work for the Father in order that, in Christ, his kingdom might come on earth as it is in heaven.

We must pray to have sufficient faith to know how to look at life . . . Grant that I may be big enough to reach the world, strong enough to carry it, pure enough to embrace it without wanting to keep it. Grant that I may be a meeting-place, but a temporary one, a road that does not end in itself, because everything to be gathered there, everything human, leads toward you.

- Father Michel Quoist

One of the reasons that hiddenness is such an important aspect of the spiritual life is that it keeps us focused on God. In hiddenness we do not receive human acclamation, admiration, support, or encouragement. In hiddenness we have to go to God with our sorrows and joys and trust that God will give us what we most need. In our society we are inclined to avoid hiddenness. We want to be seen and acknowledged. We want to be useful to others and influence the course of events. But as we become visible and popular, we grow dependent on people and their responses and easily lose touch with God, the true source of our being. Hiddenness is the place of purification . . . Even during his active ministry, Jesus continued to return to hidden places to be alone with God. If we don't have a hidden life with God, our public life for God cannot bear fruit.

- Henri Nouwen

The waves are many and the surging sea dangerous. But we are not afraid that we may be drowned, for we are standing on the rock. Let the sea rage as it will, it cannot split the rock asunder. Though the waves tower on high, they cannot overwhelm the boat of Jesus. What, pray, are we afraid of? Death? *For me, life is Christ and death is gain.* But tell me, is it exile? *The earth is the Lord's, and all it contains.* Is it the loss of property? *We brought nothing into the world. It is certain we can take nothing out of it.* The terrors of the world I despise; its treasures I deem laughable. I am not afraid of poverty, I do not long for wealth. I do not dread death.

- St. John Chrysostom

Thank you Jesus, for bringing me this far. In your light, I see the light of my life. Your teaching is brief and to the point. You persuade us to trust in our Heavenly Father. You command us to love one another. What is easier than to believe in God? What is sweeter than to love him? Your yoke is pleasant, your burden is light. You promise everything to those who obey your teaching. You ask nothing that is too hard for a believer, nothing a lover can refuse. Your promises to your disciples are true; nothing but the truth. Thank you Jesus, now and always. Amen

- St. Nicholas of Cusa

We want to know God, not merely to know that he exists . . . We want to get to know him, to appreciate his qualities and to feel at home in his presence. How are we to do that? . . . You will get to know God in proportion as you do your best, whether in your times of prayer or out of your times of prayer, to put yourself in his presence . . . Reflect that God who is Spirit is directly present to your soul which is also spirit, and that his influence manifests itself in every motion of your will, in every thought.

- Monsignor Ronald Knox

If we don't pray daily, that means if we don't look for God daily, listen for God's word daily, prepare ourselves daily for the critical trials of our life, then there would be the danger that we would slowly become blind and deaf... Pray in the every day. Rouse yourself constantly from weariness and indifference. Pray personally. Try to make a personal prayer out of everyday prayer so that you escape from the hustle and bustle around you and in you, to find you, yourself. Escape from excited haste into serenity, from the narrowness of the world into the breadth of faith, and away from self to God . . . Be lord over your emotions and moods. Pray regularly. Learn to pray. It is a grace.

- Karl Rahner

As disciples, we're asked to pick up our own cross and walk after Jesus . . . What a beautiful prayer to ask God, morning after morning, to open our ears, to open our hearts to his Word (Isaiah 50:4). And perhaps, most important of all, to give us that deep trust, that deep courage that will allow us to believe that the Lord is our help and that he is near us.

- Father Francis Michael Stiteler, O.C.S.O.

God is our all. Yet so often our aggressive daily routines shatter the delicate treasure of God's presence. Our habits are cataracts that obscure our vision. Our useless labor creates calluses that prevent us from sensing the light touch of God's hand. By daily fidelity to inner silence and solitude, the Spirit frees us from these tyrannies. In silence we allow God to till the fields of our heart. Jesus bid Lazarus wake up and Lazarus, stumbling forth from his tomb, is a concrete symbol of what each of us is called to do once we hear Christ's voice. We are to stumble forth from the tomb of lethargy, blindness, doubt and duplicity into the simple light of God's call.

- James Finley

It's true Lord that you are always thinking of us. From the beginning of time, before we existed, even before the world existed, you have been dreaming of me, thinking of me, loving me. And it is true that your love created me. It's true Lord, that you have conceived for my life a unique destiny. It's true that you have an eternal plan for me, a wonderful plan that you have always cherished in your heart, as a father thinks over the smallest of the life of his little one, still unborn. It's true that, always bending over me, you guide me to bring your plan about, light on my path and strength for my soul . . . You the divine Attentive One, you, the divine Patient One, you the divine Present One, see that at no time I forget your presence. I don't ask you to bless what I myself have decided to do, but give me the grace to discover and to live what you have dreamed for me.

- Father Michel Quoist

L et us make mercy our patroness now, and she will free us in the world to come. Yes, there is mercy in heaven but the road to it is paved by our merciful acts on earth. There is therefore, an earthly as well as a heavenly mercy. Human mercy has compassion on the miseries of the poor. Divine mercy grants forgiveness of sins. Whatever human mercy bestows here on earth, divine mercy will return to us in our Homeland . . . Yes, God who sees fit to give his mercy in heaven, wishes it to be a reality here on earth. What do you wish for, what do you pray for, my dear brothers and sisters, when you come to church? Is it mercy? How can it be anything else? . . . It baffles me that you have the impudence to ask for what you do not want to give. Give when you come to church. Give to the poor. Give them whatever your resources will allow.

- St. Caesarius of Arles

By the blessing of the Holy Spirit, you prepared my creation and my existence, not because man willed it or flesh desired it, but by your ineffable grace . . . You loved us, O Lord, and gave up your only begotten Son for our redemption . . . In this way you have humbled yourself, Christ my God, so that you might carry me, your stray sheep, on your shoulders. You let me graze in green pastures, refreshing me . . . Lord, lighten the heavy burden of the sins through which I have seriously transgressed. Purify my mind and heart. Like a shining lamp, lead me along the straight path. When I open my mouth, tell me what I should say. By the fiery tongue of your Spirit, make my own tongue ready. Stay with me always and keep me in your sight. Lead me to pastures, Lord, and graze there with me. Do not let my heart lean either to the right or to the left, but let your good Spirit guide me along the straight path. Whatever I do, let it be in accordance with your will, now until the end.

- St. John Damascene

The modern world is spiritually ill. This illness is deep, deep down in the human heart, and no one but the living Christ can heal it. In order to heal the illness of our society, Christ must be known as the Divine Physician, if he is to work the miracles of restoring ailing souls to health, and even of raising dead souls back to supernatural life. But to whom should we proclaim Christ? Absolutely speaking, we should proclaim Christ to everyone, since the Lord's mandate is clear enough. We are to make known the Good News to all creatures. We should proclaim Christ to everyone who enters our lives from this day to our dying day. Everyone.

- Father John Hardon

God is waiting to love man and to work with him. And the success of man's life depends on his finding God. Can God be found? He calls to man in the world; but the world itself is noisy, distracting and seductive. Many men in the world are concerned only with amusing themselves while waiting for death, while others, unknowing but proud, are convinced that they will somehow be able to eternalize their earthly happiness . . . If we are faithful in our meetings with Christ in daily events, little by little he will enlighten us and we will see more clearly. For Christ is less hidden than we think. Our eyes are simply not accustomed to looking at him through the darkness of our senses. Jesus Christ calls us . . . We have only to respond freely to the Savior's daily invitation.

- Father Michel Quoist

W̲e all work for results. We do not perhaps recognize the aim of our strivings at success. But we want to see our work issue in results which will gratify us and bring commendation or notice to us. We can do this even in the pursuit of holiness. But to work for results is not the same as to do God's will. This attitude of mind is due partly to our criterion of success . . . It is due partly to our pride . . . God has given us this life for one purpose, that is to prepare for the vision of him hereafter. This means that he expects us to use life to bring about a radical change within ourselves. This change involves principally that we learn to do his will because it is his will. That is holiness. Anything else is a form of self-seeking. We do not say that it is sinful, but it is selfish. And it will not sanctify us.

- Father Nivard Kinsella, O.C.S.O.

The first degree of humility tells us that the world is not a mirror in which we see ourselves, nor is it a treasure chest filled with gifts for ourselves. Rather, the world is a temporary home where there unfolds hour by hour the truth that God loves us and that we are to live constantly with the awareness that he lives with us and sees us always.

- Father Simon O'Donnell, O.S.B.

That Samaritan of ours, namely Christ . . . took pity on him (the man lying on the roadside) when he was passing the same way . . . He lifted him up from the ground, and placed him on his own mount . . . And so you must beware of ever becoming conceited about your own merits. You didn't have any, after all, when the Lord came to pick you up. In fact he found you naked, without any clothes; he found you beaten up, not in good health; he found you lying on the ground, not standing on your own feet; he discovered you straying, not returning on your own . . . You see, when you say . . . "The Lord is my guide," you will confidently be able to add, "and I will lack nothing" . . .

- St. Augustine

You must be prepared to follow Jesus generously, patiently, sometimes heroically, where he leads you . . . To love people is the one thing we have to do in their midst. Not just with any kind of love either, but with the very love that God himself bears them. We must keep repeating to ourselves untiringly that it is not only our chief work in the world but at bottom, our only work - to free and purify and increase our powers of love . . . That is what we are made for, what we are destined for. And if we are to be of any use at all in the world, it will be for having been faithful enough to allow a bit of Christ's immense love to appear through our hearts.

- Father Rene Voillaume

The healing power of the Spirit is a quiet, gentle power. He makes die in us all the fears, the desire to possess or to destroy, the hurts and the frustrations, all the power which wants to dominate. There is a growth in the power of listening, the power of compassion, of patience, of learning to wait for the hour of God. We learn to surrender to the power of the Spirit and the power of God, to stop agitating, to let God take over our lives, to abandon ourselves to the Supreme Healer . . . There is a fundamental healing that must take place before we really can listen to the music of reality, before we can listen to people without fear, before we can listen to the Spirit.

Jesus the Healer comes when we are conscious that we need a healer; when we become conscious of our own egoism, all the anarchy of desire, all the fears, all the cowardice and weakness, all the need for human security that incites us to possess. It is only when we become conscious of our weakness and our fears that we can begin to grow in union with the Spirit.

- Jean Vanier

At the end of the Sermon on the Mount, the Lord speaks to us about the two possible foundations for building the house of one's life - sand and rock. The one who builds on sand builds only on visible and tangible things - on success, on career, on money. These appear as if they are the true realities. But all this, one day will pass away. We can see this now with the fall of large financial institutions; the money disappears, it is nothing. And thus all things, which seem to be the true realities we can count on, are only realities of a secondary order. The one who builds his life on these realities, on matter, on success, on appearances, builds upon sand. Only the Word of God is the foundation of all reality; it is as stable as the heavens . . . The realist is the one who recognizes the Word of God, in this apparently weak reality, as the foundation of all things. The realist is the one who builds his life on this foundation, which is permanent.

- Pope Benedict XVI

In John's Gospel, the Lord says, I came that they may have life, and have it abundantly. Life in abundance is not as some think: to consume everything, to have all, to be able to do all that one wants. In that case we would live for inanimate things, we would live for death . . . On their return, prisoners of war who had been in Russia for ten years or more, exposed to cold and hunger, said: "I was able to survive because I knew I was expected home. I knew that people were looking forward to my return home, that I was necessary and awaited." This love that awaited them was the effective medicine of life against all ills. In reality, we are all awaited. The Lord waits for us; and not only does he wait for us, he is present and stretches out his hand to us. Let us take the Lord's hand and pray to him to grant that we may truly live, live the abundance of life.

- Pope Benedict XVI

Prayer is a gift. It is a gift because Christian prayer is based on our knowing the Lord Jesus Christ and on our having the power of the Holy Spirit that will stir and anoint us, and move through us in prayer. Prayer is based on our being part of the Body of Christ and standing with Jesus in prayer . . . We should desire prayer. We should thirst for it, seek after it, make decisions for it and repent when we don't live up to those decisions. The gift of prayer is given to us so we can be in union with God.

Prayer can transform our mind and inspire us so that in no situation, do we give way to discouragement or depression. Prayer is meant to be the assurance that we cannot be overcome. In all circumstances we can say, "I belong to God. I'm royalty. I have the first pledge of my inheritance. Regardless of what happens to me, I am in the company of the saints and the apostles and I am destined to live forever." Because of our prayer life, we are victorious.

- Father Michael Scanlan, T.O.R

B ecause you are in love with God, you can relate to him as you would relate to a friend. You can talk to him in order to find out what he thinks. You want to do as he suggests. Listen to him then, that you may know. God speaks quietly, very quietly, but he does speak, and he will make known to you what he wants you to do. To do what God wants you to do is to be truly happy. To give ourselves wholly to God, in prayer and in action, is the life of a Christian, and in it we discover joy so immense that our ordinary, everyday life is completely transformed. We find ourselves living in a new reality.

- Catherine de Hueck Doherty

What we cannot do, our Lord is able to do. Jesus Christ, perfect God and perfect man, leaves us, not a symbol, but a reality. He himself stays with us. He will go to the Father, but he will also remain among men . . . The God of our faith is not a distant being who contemplates indifferently the fate of men - their desires, their struggles, their sufferings. He is a Father who loves his children so much that he sends the Word, the Second Person of the most Blessed Trinity, so that by taking on the nature of man, he may die to redeem us. He is the loving Father who is leading us gently to himself, through the action of the Holy Spirit who dwells in our hearts.

- St. Josemaría Escrivá

I ask thee, O God, not for the goods of this world, for pleasures, for honors. Give me, by the merits of thy Passion, O my Jesus, a constant sorrow for my sins. Enlighten me and make me know the vanity of worldly goods and how much you deserve to be loved. Separate me from all attachment to the world and bind me entirely to thy love, so that from now on my will may neither seek nor desire anything but what you will. Give me patience and resignation in infirmities, in poverty, and in all those things which are contrary to my self-love. Make me gentle toward those who despise me. Give me a holy death. Give me your holy love. And above all, I pray to you to give me perseverance in your grace until death. Never permit me to separate myself from you again. And I also ask of you the grace always to have recourse to you and to invoke your aid in all my temptations. Amen

- St. Alphonsus Liguori

Lord Jesus Christ, our Savior and Redeemer, I kneel before your blessed cross. I want to open my spirit and my heart to contemplate your holy sufferings . . . May your grace be with me, the grace to shake off the coldness and indifference of my heart, to forget my everyday life for at least this half-hour, and to dwell with you in love, sorrow, and gratitude. King of all hearts, may your crucified love embrace my poor, weak, tired, and discouraged heart. Fill my heart with an interior awareness of you.

- Karl Rahner

Your business now is to live alone with God and to be as though you and God were alone in the universe. You must cross the desert and dwell in it to receive the grace of God. It is here one drives out everything that is not God. The soul needs to enter into this silence, this recollection, this forgetfulness of all created things by which God establishes his rule in it and forms within it the life of the spirit, the life of intimacy with God, the conversation of the soul with God in faith, hope and charity.

- Blessed Charles de Foucauld

Imagine Jesus crucified in your arms and on your chest, and say a hundred times as you kiss his chest, "This is my hope, the living source of my happiness; this is the heart of my soul; nothing will ever separate me from his love."

- St. Pio of Pietrelcina

God is always wanting to come closer to us, and in his eyes the whole of our span of mortal life is meant to make us accustomed to his nearness. God loves us and love is always humble and respectful; it will not force itself upon the beloved . . . All that has gone before is an attempt to show how, in our ordinary daily lives we should respond to God, surrendering to his loving concern for us and his loving will to give himself. It is not a part-time thing, it covers and must cover the whole span of our lives. It is the beginning on earth of our life in heaven. It is prayer: God incessantly giving himself, man opening himself to this gift.

- Sister Ruth Burrows, O.C.D.

Our Father in heaven, I thank you that you have led me into the light. I thank you for sending the Savior to call me from death to life. I confess that I was dead in sin before I heard his call, but when I heard him, like Lazarus, I arose. But O my Father, the grave clothes bind me still. Old habits that I cannot throw off, old customs that are so much a part of my life that I am helpless to live the new life that you call me to live. Give me strength, O Father to break the bonds; give me courage to live a new life in you.

- Anonymous

Mother Teresa and her Missionaries of Charity established one of their religious houses in the city of Rome. There they ministered to the shut-ins and the poor in the area.

On one occasion, the Sisters visited an elderly man who was in great need. They cleaned his house and cooked for him. He watched the Sisters while they worked but did not say a word. They returned the second day and performed the same service for the man. Again, the man watched the Sisters but remained silent.

On the third day, when the Sisters came to his door, he spoke to them for the first time and said, "Sisters, you have brought God into my life. Do you think you could arrange for a priest to come to my house? I want to make my confession." The man had not been to confession in more than 60 years. The Sisters were very happy and arranged for a priest to come to his home. The man made a good confession and died the following day.

OLord, all you ask of me is a simple "yes," a simple act of trust, so that your choices for me can bear fruit in my life. I do not want you to pass me by. I do not want to be so busy with my way of living, my plans and projects, my relatives, friends and acquaintances, that I do not even notice that you are with me, closer to me than anyone else. I do not want to be blind to the loving gestures that come from your hands, nor deaf to the caring words that come from your mouth. I want to see you as you walk with me and hear you as you speak to me.

-Henri Nouwen

Father, we will to share everything with your Son, his life, his divine glory, and therefore his suffering and his death. Only with the cross, give us the strength to bear it. Cause us to experience in the cross, its blessing also. Give us the cross which your wisdom knows is for our salvation and not our ruin. Son of the Father, Christ who lives in us, you are our hope of glory. Live in us, bring our life under the laws of your life, make our life like to yours. Live in me, pray in me, suffer in me, more I do not ask. For if I have you I am rich; those who find you have found the power and the victory of their life. Amen

- Karl Rahner

We make a quiet act of faith; we believe in God, we believe in God's interest in us, and we believe that he sees and hears us. We accept his will in all its details, especially in the dereliction which we experience. We put our whole reliance on the prayer of Christ of whom we are members, and with whom we have all things in common, especially his prayer; we rely on the spirit of Christ, who is within us and prays in us in an ineffable way. In other words, we quietly and gently begin to abandon ourselves, and to unite ourselves to Christ, by relying on him alone.

He is our all . . . He is working for our detachment from all creatures - even from ourselves. All his providence is directed to that end. We can be just as much attached to our spiritual goods and attainments, to our spiritual joys and powers, as we can be to the temporal. For complete union with God, and for the bearing of "more fruit" these attachments must be purged.

- Father Eugene Boylan, O.C.S.O.

Unite yourself with him, then, in all that you do. Refer everything to his glory. Set up your abode in this loving Heart of Jesus and you will there find lasting peace and the strength both to bring to fruition all the good desires he inspires in you, and to avoid every deliberate fault. Place in this Heart all your sufferings and difficulties. Everything that comes from the Sacred Heart is sweet. He changes everything into love . . . Let us belong to him without reserve, because he wants all or nothing. And after we have once given him everything, let us take nothing back.

- St. Margaret Mary Alacoque

Jesus says, *I thirst.* The Missionary of Charity should answer, "I'll quench." The quenching will cost a good deal, for to satisfy completely an infinite thirst - it will mean a continual giving, a life of sacrifice. Therefore . . . our life should be one of giving love, of giving sacrifice to God, that is - of real sacrifices made of our own free will and choice. We quench his thirst - not because we must but because we love. We must observe our vows with great love and generosity, if we wish to quench this burning thirst of God. The observance of our four vows will make us fervent religious - and fervent religious have a great power over the heart of God. If he rewards the quenching of physical thirst, think what will he not do for us, if we try to quench his own thirst - the thirst of his Heart.

- Mother Teresa of Calcutta

May your love draw down upon you the mercy of the Lord, and may he let you see that within your soul a saint is sleeping. I shall ask him to make you so open and supple that you will be able to understand and do what he wants you to do. Your life is nothing; it is not even your own. Each time you say "I'd like to do this or that," you wound Christ, robbing him of what is his. You have to put to death everything within you except the desire to love God. This is not at all hard to do. It is enough to have confidence and to thank the little Jesus for all the potentialities he has placed within you. You are called to holiness, like me, like everyone. Don't forget.

- Jacques Fesch

In the final moments of Christ's Passion, when, with pierced hands and feet, he poured out all of his precious blood on human soil to make it fruitful, lived his last hours and experienced human suffering to a greater extent than we can understand, the Gospels tell us that the earth was covered with darkness. Lord, in our lives there are also hours completely covered in darkness, sad hours in which the veil cast over our hearts hides even those things that could give us comfort, hours in which we suffer in such a way that nothing on earth can console us. Happy are those who during such times of outer darkness can still at least contemplate you, Jesus Christ, the only Life. Happy are those whose weak arms can still clasp your feet on the cross, who can lean their weary heads against your pierced hands and their bruised hearts on the heart that has suffered so much and is filled with such compassion and love.

- Elisabeth Leseur

Let us make an unconditional surrender of self to God, and seek to do a little more for him than is strictly required. Let us say, "Lord, you are enough for me; you and your cross." The cross in some form or other will always be with us. It may come from our superiors. It may come from our brethren. It may come from our body or our soul. Certainly it will come from ourselves for our self-love is our greatest cross. But let us bear all crosses cheerfully, and thank God for each.

- Father Frederic Dunne, O.C.S.O.

Praising God means to lose ourselves at his feet in words of admiration and love. It means to tell him in all the ways we know that he is infinitely perfect, infinitely worthy of love. It means to tell him over and over again and never to stop saying that he is beautiful and that we love him . . . This is the essence of prayer and the meaning of contemplation.

- Little Sister Madeleine of Jesus

I should like to bare my chest for a moment to show you the wound which our tender Jesus has lovingly opened in this heart of mine. My heart has found at last a Lover so attached to me that I am incapable of hurting him anymore . . . My heart keeps within itself an infinite number of his mercies. It knows that it doesn't have anything of value with which to glorify itself before him. He has loved me and preferred me to many others . . . He is so much in love with my heart that he makes me burn with his divine fire, with the fire of his love. What is this fire that pervades my whole being? Dear Father, if Jesus makes us so happy on earth, what will heaven be like?

- St. Pio of Pietrelcina

Someone must assure us that there is peace beyond anguish, life beyond death, and love beyond fear. It is not difficult to say to one another, "All that is good and beautiful leads us to the glory of God." However, it is difficult to say with St. Paul, *For to you has been granted, for the sake of Christ, not only to believe in him but also to suffer for him* (Phil. 1:29). Pure joy and sorrow are no longer opposites, but have become the two sides of the same desire to grow in the fullness of Jesus Christ.

- Father Augustine Moore, O.C.S.O.

Unless the Lord builds the house, the builders labor in vain. You are the temple of God. This is the house and temple of God, full of his doctrine and his power, a dwelling place holy enough to house the heart of God . . . Such a temple must be built by God; if it were constructed by human effort, it would not last; it is not held together by resting on merely worldly teachings, nor will it be protected by our own vain efforts or anxious concern. We must build it and protect it in a different way. It must not have its foundations on earth or on sand that is unstable and treacherous. Its foundations must be rooted in the prophets and apostles. It must be built up from living stones, held together by a cornerstone; an ever increasing unity will make it grow into a perfect humanity, to the scale of Christ's body . . . A house so built by God, that is by God's guidance, will not collapse. Through the efforts of the individual faithful, this house will grow into many houses, and thus will arise the blessed and spacious city of God.

- St. Hilary of Poitiers

The wilderness or desert, formed the backdrop for the prophets, the Psalms, and the Exodus. John the Baptist preached in the wilderness, and the Spirit drove Jesus into the wilderness to be tempted . . . The Spirit urges us to seek time alone with God . . . Our desert and wilderness can be a meaningless job, chronic illness, a crumbling relationship, or the loss of a loved one.

Whatever wilderness we travel into, God is ever inviting us to depend on the love poured out in Jesus . . . In the midst of the desert, we might grumble and rebel . . . We might temporarily abandon the God who truly liberates us from our slavery, the God who loves us totally. God understands this rebellion and anger as our attempt to control our own destiny, to call all the shots. God trusts that once we have faced the desert, confronted the reality of our vulnerability, we will rush into the Divine embrace.

- Wayne Simsic

Shake off all earthly things, counting them useless, noxious, and hurtful to you. When you have done this, enter wholly within yourself, and fix your gaze upon the wounded Jesus, and upon him alone. Strive with all your powers, to reach God through himself, that is through God made man, that you may attain to the knowledge of his divinity through the wounds of his sacred humanity.

- St. Albert the Great

What we are trying to do is to realize that, while we are on earth, faith places us in the heat of battle. We are in a permanent struggle, a constant choice between Jesus Christ and that which in the world, remains hostile to God. This struggle is to accomplish within ourselves the Church's own vocation. On the earth, the Church is made for fighting. By her vocation, she wages war against evil. By her mission, she stands on the front lines against evil. By her office, she delivers from evil . . . The place that Christian hope assigns to the Church, to us, is that narrow ridge, that borderline, at which our vocation requires that we choose, every day and every hour, to be faithful to God's faithfulness to us.

- Madeleine Delbrel

Christianity is more about our undoing than our pulling it together. It's the unraveling of our grandiose plans. The collapsing of our defenses. The slow release of the reins in our tightly clenched fists. The seed falling to the ground to die. The failure to build a mighty tower reaching to heaven. For every few steps we progress, God reveals how many miles we have yet to go. So let us persevere in offering a sacrifice of surrender, for the salvation of our own souls and for those around us.

- Anonymous

Jesus was broken on the cross. He lived his suffering and death not as an evil to avoid at all costs but as a mission to embrace. We too are broken. We live with broken bodies, broken hearts, broken minds, or broken spirits. We suffer from broken relationships. How can we live our brokenness? Jesus invites us to embrace our brokenness as he embraced the cross and live it as a part of our mission. He asks us not to reject our brokenness as a curse from God that reminds us of our sinfulness but to accept it and put it under God's blessing for our purification and sanctification. Thus our brokenness can become a gateway to a new life.

- Henri Nouwen

All of us will die on a day we do not know at present, but how happy we will be if we die with our dear Savior in our hearts. Indeed, we must always keep him there, making our spiritual exercises in his company and offering him our desires, resolutions and protests. It is a thousand times better to die with the Lord than to live without him . . . If the death of the Savior is propitious for us, our own death will be a happy one. For this reason we should often think of his holy death, and love his Cross and his Passion.

- St. Francis de Sales

God put you into the world to offer your whole life as a sacrifice to him in union with the perfect sacrifice of our Lord Jesus Christ. He knows the handicaps you started with. Of course he does, because it was he who put them there . . . He meant those handicaps to be the condition of the sacrifice you were to offer to him. When he became man on earth, he might have been the son of an emperor, but he became the son of a carpenter. It wasn't bad luck. He preferred it that way because it made his sacrifice more perfect. And every disadvantage you started life with is, in the same way, part of his plan. It is to make your sacrifice to him more perfect.

- Monsignor Ronald Knox

It is Jesus that you seek when you dream of happiness; he is waiting for you when nothing else you find satisfies you; he is the beauty to which you are so attracted; it is he who provokes you with that thirst for fulfillment that will not let you settle for compromise; it is he who urges you to shed the masks of a false life . . . It is Jesus who stirs in you the desire to do something great with your lives, the will to follow an ideal, the refusal to allow yourselves to be ground down by mediocrity, the courage to commit yourselves humbly and patiently to improving yourselves and society, making the world more human and more fraternal.

- Pope John Paul II

Let your thought always be upward toward God, and direct your prayers continually to Christ. If you cannot, because of your frailty, always occupy your mind in contemplation of God, yet be occupied with a remembrance of his Passion, and make yourself a dwelling place in his blessed wounds. And if you flee devoutly to the wound in Christ's side, and to the marks of his Passion, you will feel great comfort in every trouble.

- Thomas à Kempis

Prayer never touches us as long as it remains on the surface of our lives, as long as it is nothing but one more of the thousand things that must be done. It is only when prayer becomes "the one thing necessary" that real prayer begins . . . We are called upon to live Christ's life. We are called into the desert . . . We are called to face God alone in the night of our own solitude. We are called to die with Jesus, in order to live with him. We are asked to lose all, to be emptied out, in order to be filled with the very fullness of God . . . Christianity is much more than an expression of brotherly love couched in religious terms. It is essential that each person make some kind of personal response to God in Christ.

- James Finley

Oh Jesus, will you one day put my poor soul and my poor life also into the hands of the Father? Put everything there - the burden of my life, and the burden of my sins, not on the scales of justice, but into the hands of the Father. Where should I flee, where should I seek refuge, if not at your side? For you are my brother in bitter moments, and you suffered for my sins . . . See, I come to you today. I kneel beneath your cross. I kiss the feet which follow me down the wandering path of my life constantly and silently . . . I embrace your cross, Lord of Eternal Love, Heart of all Hearts, Heart that was pierced, Heart that is patient and unspeakably kind. Have mercy on me. Receive me into your love. And when I come to the end of my pilgrimage, when the day begins to decline and the shadows of death surround me, speak your last word at the end of my life also: *Father, into your hands I commend his spirit.*

- Karl Rahner

Living within the truth means living according to Jesus Christ and God's Word in Sacred Scripture. It means proclaiming the truth of the Christian Gospel . . . It means believing that the truths of the Creed are worth suffering and dying for. Living within the truth also means telling the truth and calling things by their right names. And that means exposing the lies by which some men try to force others to live . . . We are ambassadors of the living God to a world that is on the verge of forgetting him. Our work is to make God real; to be the face of his love. . .so that when we make our accounting to the Lord, we will be numbered among the faithful and courageous, and not the cowardly or the evasive, or those who compromised until there was nothing left of their convictions; or those who were silent when they should have spoken the right word at the right time.

- Archbishop Charles J. Chaput

Most of Christ's earthly life was hidden. He was hidden in his mother's womb, he was hidden in Egypt and in Nazareth. During his public life he was hidden often, when he fled into "a mountain to pray." During the forty days of his risen life, again and again he disappeared and hid himself from men. Today he is hidden in the Blessed Sacrament, in Heaven, and in his mystical body on earth. But in his Passion he was exposed, made public property to the whole of mankind. The last time he went up into a mountain to pray, it was to pray out loud, in a voice that would echo down the ages, ringing in the ears of mankind forever. It was to be stripped naked before the whole world, forever, not only in body, but in mind and soul . . . Every detail of his Passion revealed something more of his character as man. Not only his heroism and his majesty, but his human necessities, and the human limitations which he deliberately adopted as part of his plan of love, in order to be able to indwell in us as we are, with our limitations and psychological as well as physical necessities and interdependence on one another.

- Caryll Houselander

If you lose the supernatural meaning of your life, your charity will be philanthropy; your purity, decency; your mortification, stupidity; your discipline, a whip; and all your works, fruitless.

- St. Josemaría Escrivá

We must live with the expectations that other people have in our lives . . . While we all hear many voices in our lives, it is critical to our spiritual health that we listen first and foremost to the voice of Jesus Christ. The goal of our lives is not to meet the expectations of our parents, friends, spouses, children and others. We are called to follow Jesus Christ and carry out his mission of love, generosity and compassion in this world.

Lent is a great time to refocus our attention on Jesus - to listen to him through the teachings of the church, through scripture, and through our service. Lent is a time to listen to our own experience to try to discern the voice of God amid all the other voices that we hear each day. And Lent also challenges us to avoid letting any other person or institution take the place of God in our lives. No matter how well intended our friends and family are, they are not God. Jesus is God's son. The challenge of Lent is to listen to him.

- Bill Peatman

God could put me here. He could put me there. He can use me. He cannot use me. It doesn't matter because I belong so totally to him that he can do just what he wants to do with me. Lent is a time when we relive the Passion of Christ. Let it not be just a time when our feelings are roused, but let it be a change that comes through cooperation with God's grace in real sacrifices of self. Sacrifice to be real, must cost; it must hurt; it must empty us of self. Let us go through the Passion of Christ day by day.

- Mother Teresa of Calcutta

You are the stones of the Father's temple, made ready for God's building. . .Your faith pulls you upwards and love is the way that raises you to God. You are all to be companions on this road, bearers of God, temples of the Spirit, carriers of Christ, bringing with you holy gifts. You are adorned by the commandments of Jesus Christ . . . Nothing is hidden from the Lord, even our secrets are close to him. So as we go about our work let us always remember that he dwells in us: so we will be his temples, and he will be our God present in us . . . It is precisely as we love him that he will show himself to us.

- St. Ignatius of Antioch

Jesus on the cross said these beautiful and sad words, *I am thirsty* (John 19:28). Since then, throughout the ages, all of humanity has echoed these words . . . Now, O God, with all my heart, I say the sorrowful words, "I am thirsty." I am thirsty for the peace you alone give, which transforms life; for the stability and living refreshment that only exists in you. I am thirsty for light, thirsty to know, to see, to possess, as we shall see and possess in eternity. I am thirsty for the profound sensitivity and the tenderness that can read hearts, and for a close and strong union with you . . . I am thirsty for immortality, that complete flourishing of the soul beyond this transitory world. I am thirsty for life, the only Life, abundant and eternal, with all our loves restored in the heart of infinite Love. My God, I am thirsty for you.

- Elisabeth Leseur

Humility is a supernatural virtue by which we lovingly recognize our true value in God's eyes, and are disposed to render him due recognition for all the good we find in ourselves . . . We are the soil in which Christ grows; his roots will only pick out from us what is in accordance with his Father's will. Therefore it depends upon us to decide whether by doing the will of God we are to be absorbed by Christ and are to enter into life - or to be left by him in the exterior darkness of our own will.

- Father Eugene Boylan, O.C.S.O.

I consider what writers say about the kingfishers, little birds who build their nests on the beach near the sea. They build it in a circular form and so tightly compressed that the sea water cannot penetrate it . . . Here these graceful little birds place their young ones, so that when the sea comes upon them by surprise, they can swim with confidence and float on the waves . . . I want your heart to be like this: well-compact and closed on all sides, so that if the worries and storms of the world, the evil spirit, and the flesh come upon it, it will not be penetrated. Leave but one opening to your heart, that is toward heaven . . . How I love and am enraptured by those little birds.

- St. Pio of Pietrelcina

Today we are all well aware that the word "heaven" does not designate a place beyond the stars but something much greater and more difficult to express, namely, that God has a place for us and that God gives us eternity . . . God never passes away, and we all exist because he loves us, because he brought us into existence by his creative act. His love is the foundation of our eternity. . .It is his love that makes us immortal, and this immortality, this abiding love, is what we call "heaven." Heaven, then, is none other than the certainty that God is great enough to have room even for us . . . Nothing that we treasure or value will be destroyed. As we ponder all this, let us ask the Lord on this day to open our eyes ever more fully to it; to make us not only people of faith but also people of hope, who do not look to the past but rather build for today and tomorrow a world that is open to God.

- Pope Benedict XVI

Finally, however, I ask you for the hardest and most difficult, for the grace to recognize the Cross of your Son in all the suffering of my life, to adore your holy and inscrutable will in it, to follow your Son on his way to the cross as long as it may please you. Make me sensitive to what concerns your honor and not merely my own well being, and then I also will be able to carry many a cross as atonement for my sins. Do not let me be embittered by suffering but mature, patient, selfless, gentle, and filled with longing for that land where there is no pain, and for that day when you will wipe all tears from the eyes of those who have loved you, and in sorrow have believed in your love, and in darkness have believed in your light. Let my pain be a profession of my faith in your promises, a profession of my hope in your goodness and fidelity, a profession of my love, that I love you more than myself, that I love you for your own sake, even without reward . . . Grant us to become so mature in true Christian being and life that we no longer regard the cross as a misfortune . . . but as a sign of your election, as the secret, sure sign that we are yours forever.

- *Karl Rahner*

To the ancient Hebrews, life meant far more than the period between conception and death. Life was what proceeded from loving and obeying God. And death was not just that which followed the last breath on earth. To the ancient Hebrews, death was the rejection of the living God. *Seek the Lord and you will live*, the prophet Amos tells the people. And, conversely, isolate yourself from the love of the Lord, and you will join the living dead. The point is that you and I are not genuinely alive because we are not medically dead. We are genuinely alive when our actions are full of love and understanding and intelligence and heart. To be genuinely alive, we must experience God. It is not enough to know about God. We must know him, experience him. We can only know him and experience him through love. The first letter of John states, *Whoever does not love, does not know God* . . . When we consider all things through the love of Christ, we are alive in Christ. St. Paul puts it this way, *For to me, to live is Christ.* Today we pray for the strength to be fully alive, and the grace to choose the life of Christ.

- Father Joseph Pellegrino

Christ, who identified himself with sinners . . . turned to sinners as much as to saints for help. He was grateful for the help of the thief on the cross, the generosity of this derelict, dying man who acknowledged Christ's goodness when those who knew him well had fled. Even when he was dead, he accepted his tomb, the place where his body should rest, from Nicodemus, the hesitating, careful man who dared only to come to him under cover of darkness. There is no exemption from the love of Christ in one another, or from sharing the cross. There is no moment when, if we meet one whose burden is too heavy, we may delay in helping to carry it. It is not for those who are good alone to help Christ; it is most of all for sinners, for the weak, the hesitating, even the selfish . . . Every day, hidden under our sins, abject in his need, Christ says to the sinners who put out a hand or speak a word to help him, *This day you shall be with me in Paradise.*

- Caryll Houselander

I must always be conscious of Jesus' humanity. I must realize that my sorrows are akin to his, that my difficulties are such that he will understand them; that, although his strength is divine and is upheld by God, his compassion is thereby not less human; that he is God indeed from all eternity, but man as truly from the moment of the Incarnation; man to understand by experience, God to help us; man to suffer and die, God, that death and suffering may have infinite avail . . . There is a real relationship of love between me and Jesus' humanity.

- Father Bede Jarrett

We must ask ourselves what burdens us, what weighs us down, and keeps us from spiritually moving forward. The cross is not so heavy that we cannot carry it or move under its weight . . . But if you are burdened by the weight of this world's glitter and gold, you will soon be immobilized by it. It will not only weigh you down, it will crush you . . . We bury ourselves in outsized houses, cars, boats, computers, TV's, and all manner of other things . . . The secular world's religion is one of getting, acquiring, buying, and filling one's life with more and more things . . . Jesus on the Cross is a sign of contradiction, a sign that contradicts the message of the world that surrounds us. It is also a sign of liberation, of freedom. The Cross tells us that if we live life as Jesus did, if we live in his way, his truth and his life, we will find freedom that the world cannot give.

- Father Charles Irvin

Your sole concern should be the establishment of God's reign in your heart, in this life and in the next. In this life your study should be to bring about this reign of God, in your heart by his grace and through the plentitude of his love. You should live for God alone, and the life of your soul should be the life of God himself. You ought likewise to nourish yourself with God by thinking of his holy presence as often as you possibly can. That which constitutes the life of the saints is precisely their continual attention to God and this also should form the life of those who . . . seek only to accomplish his holy will, to love him and so make others love him.

- St. John Baptiste de la Salle

Hence, the apostles say that this mystical wisdom is revealed by the Holy Spirit. If you ask how such things can occur, seek the answer in God's grace, not in doctrine; in the longing of the will, not in the understanding; in the sighs of prayer, not in research; seek the Bridegroom not the teacher; God and not man . . . Let us pass over with the crucified Christ from this world to the Father so that, when the Father has shown himself to us, we can say with Philip, *It is enough.* We may hear with Paul, *My grace is sufficient for you,* and we can rejoice with David, saying, *My flesh and my heart fail me, but God is the strength of my heart and my heritage forever.*

- *St. Bonaventure*

For me, there is no greater image than the Holy Face of Jesus because it embodies the physical and spiritual suffering of Christ, the Redeemer. In the Holy Face, the sick person sees how suffering can and should be accepted. By imploring the Lord to sanctify his suffering and make it similar to Jesus', it becomes redemptive for the soul and purifying for one's existence . . . The Holy Face of Jesus is beautiful. Look at it.

- Cardinal Fiorenzo Angelini

Jesus, you have told us many times, in many different ways, to trust in you, to have faith in you. If you had not given us that gift of faith, we would be wandering on the earth, looking for you without knowing what we are looking for. We would have been empty people, ghostly people. We treasure that gift despite all of our fickleness and all of our weakness . . . And though we have failed in so many ways, so many times, we trust in your love and forgiveness; we trust that you will renew our faith and let us be yours in every way, now and forever.

- Father Killian Speckner

We know for certain that Our Lady was at the side of Jesus at the Crucifixion . . . Let's ask him, through her prayers, to accept our lives and our deaths as a sacrifice in union with his own, in reparation for our sins and for all the sins of the world. Let's ask her to make our hearts tender towards other people's misfortunes, treating the tragedies of the world as our own and eager to lighten them as far as that is in our power. Let's ask that the spear which wounded Jesus may open our hearts to the love of God and to the love of our neighbor.

- Monsignor Ronald Knox

Faith is not a thing of the mind; it is not an intellectual certainty or a felt conviction of the heart. It is a sustained decision to take God with utter seriousness as the God of my life. It is to live out each hour in a practical, concrete affirmation that God is Father and he is "in heaven." It is a decision to shift the center of our lives from ourselves to him, to forego self-interest and make his interests, his will, our sole concern. This is what it means to hallow his name as our Father in heaven . . . All that matters to faith is that God should have what he wants and we know that what he wants is always our own blessedness. His purposes are worked out, his will is mediated to us, in the humblest form, as humble as our daily bread.

- Sister Ruth Burrows, O.C.D.

Lord, I called for you in my longing to enjoy your dear company; for your sake I am ready to give up all else. It was you who first moved me to seek you; bless you, Lord, for doing your servant this kindness in your unbounded mercy. What more can your servant say to you? . . .Yes, there is nothing to compare with you out of all the wonders of heaven and earth. All your works are good, all your judgments are true; your providence is at the helm of all creation. Let praise and glory be yours, then O Wisdom of the Father; let my lips, my soul and the whole of creation together praise you and bless you.

- Thomas à Kempis

Psalmody (praying the psalms) is one of the traditional roads to the experience of God . . . So we say the psalms with Jesus, all of them, in the long quiet years of manual work, in the solitary days in the desert on Tabor and in Galilee, walking on the sea and preaching on the hillside, with him on his way to the Holy City, in his struggles with the world, with law and authority, with the establishment, with him in his betrayal, his suffering and death . . . in his glorious rising, until he comes again at the end. Praying with him in the wilderness of this world, unafraid, rooted in faith and in his love.

- Father Matthew Kelty, O.C.S.O.

If only we could actuate this right thinking in answering our daily calls, we would widen a spiritual horizon, a vista so beautiful . . . He is asking for patience, that we may come to him who bore all our infirmities without complaint . . . He is offering an opportunity for meekness and humility, that we may deepen our communication with Jesus, who is meek and humble of heart . . . This is what we mean by "call." Not a call to do this or to do that, to suffer this or to give up that, but always a call to come to God. Thus we come to pray, "In the hour of my death, call me," knowing that he will, and for the same reason that he has called me all during my life: that I may come to him . . . When God calls us, it is for a reason, particularly in that dearest final call, which will be made because he just wants to see us. We can help one another remember, by our manner of living, that God has always the same elemental reason for each of his calls, whether in life or death: that we may come to him. This is what we want to do: understand every call.

- Mother Mary Francis, P.C.C.

I don't believe that my life is a long row of randomly chained incidents and accidents of which I am not much more than a passive victim. No, I think that nothing is accidental but that God molded me through the events of my life and that I am called to recognize his molding hand and praise him in gratitude for the great things he has done for me. I wonder if I really have listened carefully enough to the God of history, the God of my history, and have recognized him when he called me by my name . . . Maybe I have been living much too fast, too restlessly, too feverishly, forgetting to pay attention to what is happening here and now . . . Just as a whole world of beauty can be discovered in one flower, so the great grace of God can be tasted in one small moment.

- Henri Nouwen

We must try to be children who realize that the Lord is such a good Father, by loving us as his children, he has taken us into his house, in the middle of the world . . . Our Father in heaven pardons any offense when his child returns to him, when he repents and asks for pardon. The Lord is such a good Father that he anticipates our desire to be pardoned and comes forward to us, opening his arms laden with grace . . . He wants us to call him Father; he wants us to savor that word, our souls filled with joy. Human life is in some way a constant returning to our Father's house.

- Josemaría Escrivá

B e devoted to God and do not fear, for no harm can come to those who follow Christ. Even if they take away the life of your body, Christ is still with you . . . Nobody can teach you better than the Church how you are to keep Christ with you . . . He is held by the mind knowing him, and by the heart loving him. So if you want to hold Christ, seek him constantly and do not fear . . . One who seeks Christ and finds him can say with the scriptures, *I will never leave him, never let him go till I have brought him into my mother's house.* What is this room except the inner secret room of your own person? Keep this inner room clean, so that when it is pure, unstained by sin, your spiritual home may stand as a priestly temple with the Holy Spirit dwelling in it. One who seeks and entreats Christ is never abandoned, but visited by him frequently, for he is always with us.

- St. Ambrose

The Apostle tells us to rejoice, but in the Lord, not in the world. Whoever wishes to be a friend of this world, says scripture, will be reckoned as enemy of God. As a man cannot serve two masters, so one cannot rejoice both in the world and in the Lord. Let joy in the Lord prevail, then, until joy in the world is no more. Let joy in the Lord go on increasing; let joy in the world go on decreasing until it is no more . . . So, brethren, rejoice in the Lord not in the world. That is, rejoice in the truth, not in wickedness; rejoice in the hope of eternity, not in the fading flower of vanity. That is the way to rejoice. Wherever you are on earth, however long you remain on earth, the Lord is near; do not be anxious about anything.

- St. Augustine

Go through the motions of praying, if that is all you can do, and when you have finished, offer it up to God in a spirit of great humility. Tell him that he knows your fashioning, knows you are but dust; deplore the natural weakness which makes it so hard for you, his creature, to do the thing you were put into the world to do. Confess to him, at the same time, the habitual want of seriousness and purpose in your life which prevents you attaining recollection when you want it. Tell him you wish your prayer had been one long peaceful aspiration to him; unite it with the prayer of our Blessed Lord while he was on earth, and ask to have it accepted with that mantle cast over it. Offer to God your will, the will that is so weak, and has achieved so little. Then perhaps this distracted prayer of yours may be more acceptable to God than the most fervent prayer you ever offered in your life. He wants us to throw ourselves at his feet.

- Monsignor Ronald Knox

God himself says: *I have loved thee with an everlasting love* . . . He is our Savior; that is something that must never be forgotten. And it is as our Savior, that he enters into partnership with us. In fact, it is by that very partnership that he saves us. He comes to us full of perfect knowledge and unlimited love. He knows exactly what we are, and he knows exactly what our life will be. He knows all our defects and weaknesses, those that are natural to us, those that are the result of circumstances, and those that are the result of our own sins. He knows all that has happened or will happen to us. He knows all that might have been done for us or by us, but which has been neglected. He knows all our mistakes and all our sins; He knows all our misfortunes and all our miseries. He knows all these things in advance, but being the perfect Lover, he comes with the power of God to heal all these ills. He is perfectly prepared to repair our life completely if we do not prevent him.

- Father Eugene Boylan, O.C.S.O.

Worldly people have not the Holy Spirit, or if they have, it is only for a moment . . . the noise of the world drives him away. A Christian who is led by the Holy Spirit has no difficulty in leaving the goods of this world, to run after those of heaven; he knows the difference between them. The eyes of the world see no further than this life . . . The eyes of the Christian see deep into eternity . . . We must therefore find out by whom we are led. If it is not by the Holy Spirit, we labor in vain.

- St. John Vianney

For the Christian living in the world, real prayer is that which goes before action, and is its necessary concomitant. Human action is for God, what water is in baptism, and bread in the Eucharist; the material for divine operation. We cannot do without prayer, but it must be prolonged in action. I ought to plead to God for my neighbor in danger, but I should also hold out a hand to save him from drowning. The same Master who told us to pray without ceasing, commanded us also to go out and act.

- Cardinal Leo Joseph Suenens

The kingdom of God is within you (Luke 17:21). From this we learn that by a heart made pure . . . we see in our own beauty, the image of the Godhead . . . You have within you the ability to see God. He who formed you, put into your being an immense power. When God created you, he enclosed in you the image of his perfection, as the mark of a seal is impressed on wax. But your straying has obscured God's image . . . You are like a metal coin . . . The coin was dirty, but now it reflects the brightness of the sun and shines in its turn. So when people look at themselves, they will see within themselves the One they are seeking. And this is the joy that will fill their purified hearts.

- St. Gregory of Nyssa

It is always an illusion to think that one has been converted once and for all . . . Conversion always has something to do with time. A human being needs time, and God wants to take time with us . . . Human beings are so created that they need time to grow, to mature, to develop their full potential. God knows this much better than we do. For that reason he waits. He does not stop caring; he is long suffering and patient . . . So every day God works with us, calling us to repentance: *Oh that today you would hear his voice: harden not your hearts* (Psalm 95:7). God speaks in various ways. He speaks through his Word, through the people with whom we live, through all sorts of circumstances, joyful and painful. We dread the latter especially. We know all too well that God has something to say to us in affliction, sickness, death or misfortune . . . for it is God who comes to touch us in countless ways to teach us conversion.

- Father Andre Louf, O.C.S.O.

Driven out of Paradise by you and exiled in a distant land, I cannot return by myself unless you, O Lord, come to meet me in my wandering. My return is based on hope in your mercy during all of my earthly life. My only hope, the only source of confidence, and the only solid promise is your mercy.

- St. Augustine

John's Gospel tells us that after the Resurrection the Lord went to his disciples, breathed upon them and said, *Receive the Holy Spirit* . . .We can say, therefore, that the Holy Spirit is the breath of Jesus Christ and we in a certain sense, must ask Christ to breathe on us always, so that his breath will become alive . . . this means that we must keep close to Christ. We do so by meditating on his Word. We know that the principal author of the Sacred Scriptures is the Holy Spirit . . . and then, naturally, this listening, walking in the environment of the Word, must be transformed into a response - a response in prayer, in contact with Christ.

- Pope Benedict XVI

Jesus is the Savior of the world. We are not. We are called to witness, always with our lives and sometimes with our words, to the great things God has done for us . . . When we think about Jesus we mostly think about his words and miracles, his passion, death and resurrection, but we should never forget that before all of that, Jesus lived a simple, hidden life in a small town, far away from all the great people, great cities, and great events. Jesus' hidden life is very important for our own spiritual journey. If we want to follow Jesus by words and deeds in the service of his kingdom, we must first of all strive to follow Jesus in his simple, unspectacular, and very ordinary hidden life.

- Henri Nouwen

Christ gives us his risen life, he rises in us, if we become sharers in his cross and his death. We should love the cross, self-sacrifice and mortification. Christian optimism is not something sugary, nor is it a human optimism that things will "work out well." No, its deep roots are awareness of freedom and faith in grace. It is an optimism which makes us demanding of ourselves. It gets us to make a real effort to respond to God's call. Not so much despite our wretchedness but in some ways through it, through our life as men of flesh and blood and dust, Christ is shown forth; in our effort to be better, to have a love which wants to be pure, to overcome our selfishness, to give ourselves fully to others - to turn our existence into a continuous service.

- St. Josemariá Escrivá

Let us remind ourselves over and over again that holiness has to do with very ordinary things: truthfulness, courtesy, kindness, gentleness, consideration for others, contentment with our lot, honesty and courage in the face of life, reliability, dutifulness . . . If we were to offer advice to those who want to advance . . . it would be to set the compass, so to speak; to aim at this gathering up of the self so as to be able to give that self to God. This has nothing to do with a psychic awareness, it happens in day to day life. It involves constant watchfulness for the call of God so as to answer with an immediate "yes." We miss countless opportunities when he is there offering himself because we don't notice him, we are not really looking for him. This is where our attention should be - the whole of it - on noticing where he is, what he is asking now, not on spiritual states, stages, what happens to us when we are at prayer, what we feel of God and all the rest of it. What matters is that at every moment of our life we are there, waiting, receptive.

- Sister Ruth Burrows, O.C.D.

Let our prayers ascend to Mary in this month of hers (May), to implore her graces and favors with increased fervor and confidence. And if the grave faults of men weigh heavy in the scales of God's justice and provoke its just punishments, we also know that the Lord is *"the Father of mercies and the God of all comfort"* (Cor 2: 1:3) and that Mary most holy is his appointed steward and the generous bestower of the treasures of his mercy. May she, who knows the sufferings and troubles of life here below, the weariness of everyday work, the hardships and privations of poverty, the sufferings of Calvary, bring help to the needs of the Church and the world, heed the appeals for peace rising to her from every part of the world, and enlighten those who rule the destinies of men. May she prevail on God, Lord of the winds and storms, to still also the tempests in men's conflicting hearts and "grant us peace in our day," true peace based on the solid lasting foundations of justice and love of justice granted to the weakest as to the strongest; and love which prevents egoism from leading men astray, so that each one's rights may be safeguarded without forgetfulness or denial of the rights of others.

- Pope Paul VI

My Lord, I have no hope but in your Cross. You, by your humility, sufferings and death, have delivered me from all vain hope. You have killed the vanity of the present life in yourself and have given me all that is eternal in rising from the dead. My hope is in what the eye has never seen. Therefore let me not trust in visible rewards. My hope is in what the human heart cannot feel. Therefore let me not trust in the feelings of my heart. My hope is in what the hand has never touched. Do not let me trust what I can grasp between my fingers, because death will loosen my grasp and my vain hope will be gone. Let my trust be in your mercy, not in myself. Let my hope be in your love, not in health or strength or ability or human resources. If I trust you, everything else will become for me strength, health and support. Everything will bring me to heaven. If I do not trust you, everything will be my destruction.

- Father Thomas Merton, O.C.S.O.

I recommend that you give an hour each day to personal prayer - to being with him whom we know loves us. It is in this kind of prayer that the Holy Spirit can impart interior peace, which enables us to endure in the face of overwhelming and unsolvable problems . . . And so, in a difficult time we should not forget that the great works of God have been accomplished in darkness. The people fled Egypt in the darkness; they crossed the Red Sea in the darkness; the Lord Jesus was born in Bethlehem in the darkness of night; he gave us the Eucharist and the priesthood in the darkness of the Last Supper; he died on the Cross when the Gospel says, darkness covered the earth. He lay in the darkness of the tomb. On the third day, he rose again in the darkness, and the empty tomb was discovered "early in the morning while it was still dark." God is at work even in the darkness.

- Archbishop John Quinn

For many years now God has been watching over this city, ever on the alert. He cared for Abraham in his wanderings; he rescued Isaac when he was about to be sacrificed; Jacob, he enriched in his time of servitude; it is he who set Joseph over Egypt after he had been sold into slavery; who supported Moses against Pharaoh; chose Joshua to lead his nation in war; rescued David from every peril; and endowed Solomon with wisdom. He came to the aid of the prophets, he took Elijah up to heaven, chose Elisha; fed Daniel, and stood by and refreshed the three young men in the fiery furnace. He told Joseph through an angel, of his virginal conception, he strengthened Mary, and sent John ahead to prepare the way. He chose the apostles and prayed for them, saying to his Father, *Father most holy, protect them. While I was with them, I kept them safe by the power of your name.* Finally, after his Passion, he promised us his eternal, watchful protection, in the words, *Behold I am with you always until the end of the world.* Such is the never failing protection given to this blessed and holy city, a city built for God . . . It is therefore the Lord who must build this city if it is to grow to its appointed size.

- *St. Hilary of Poitiers*

We must persevere in quiet meditation on the life, sayings, deeds, sufferings and death of Jesus in order to learn what God promises and what he fulfills. One thing is certain: we must always live close to the presence of God, for that is newness of life, and then nothing is impossible for all things are possible with God; no earthly power can touch us without his will, and danger can only drive us closer to him. We can claim nothing for ourselves, and yet we may pray for everything. Our joy is hidden in suffering, our life in death. But all through, we are sustained in a wondrous fellowship . . . In these turbulent times we are always forgetting what it is that makes life really worthwhile. We think that life has a meaning for us so long as such and such a person still lives. But the truth is that if this earth was good enough for the man Jesus Christ, if a man like him really lived in it, then, and only then, has life a meaning for us.

- Dietrich Bonhoeffer

Before the tabernacle: Lord, I want to thank you for your presence . . . in this house, the house of your Father, and for dwelling within it, so as not to be distant and hidden from us with the Father and the Spirit, but rather to remain among us as the way that leads to the Father . . . Lord, you know how weak and distracted we are and how we consider everything else more important than you; but again and again you guide us back to this place where you dwell in order to change us.

- Hans Urs von Balthasar

Many things are given to us through the Holy Spirit, but they are valueless if the chief gift of charity is lacking . . . Even if all the other gifts are lacking, charity will take us to the kingdom of God. Although faith can exist without charity, only the faith that works through love can have any value. The Holy Spirit is the charity of the Father and the Son, by means of which they love each other . . . When he is given to men, he enkindles in their hearts the love of God and of their fellow men . . . It is he who teaches us to pray as we ought, making us cleave to God . . . He enlightens our minds and forms love in our hearts. All of this is the work of the Holy Spirit.

- William of St. Thierry

To share Christ's resurrection means not to be shackled by temporal things but to set our hearts on the eternal life he is offering us here and now . . . St. Paul tells us to *make no provision for the flesh, to gratify its desires* . . . But we must now take care of our bodies for the sake of serving the Lord, not for the sake of indulging ourselves. We are a new creation in Christ Jesus . . . Christ has made us his members, and we have acknowledged him as our Lord and Savior. Now that we have begun to live a new life in him, let us take care not to return to our former useless existence. We have put our hands to the plow; we must not give up or look nostalgically at what we have left behind, but keep our attention on what we are sowing. It would be the greatest tragedy to fall back again into the hopelessness from which the Lord Jesus has raised us up.

- St. Leo the Great

By justice, Jesus Christ once risen should have ascended at once to the glory of the right hand of the Father . . . And yet we know very well that for forty days he wanted to be seen as risen. And why? To affirm, as St. Leo says, by such an excellent mystery, the good news of our faith . . . These forty days before our ascent to heaven will pass for us too. Perhaps they will not be days, but months and years. I wish you, my brothers and sisters, a long and prosperous life full of heavenly and material blessings. But finally this life will come to an end. And then we will be happy, if we have assured for ourselves the joy of a happy transit to eternity. Then our resurrection will be complete. There will be no more danger of losing the grace of God. There will no longer be any suffering, no more death, but instead everlasting life with our Savior, Jesus Christ in heaven. May the Lord confirm with his blessings these wishes of mine, for your happiness is very close to my heart and I work and pray continuously for this end.

- St. Pio of Pietrelcina

We are permitted to love our relations, our possessions, our health, our reputation; but this love must be subordinate to the love we should have for God, so that we should be ready to make the sacrifice of it if he should require it.

- St. John Vianney

When we profess our belief in eternal life, it is a profession of faith in the living God. Because there is a God, we, whom he calls and sees, know that we shall not fall into a vacuum. For that reason, belief in eternal life becomes a very practical testimony. . .It is right and necessary to remind us that the measure of human life is what we call eternity. . . and that human beings have souls that do not die with their bodies, but are bearers of the good news of God's life and of the Resurrection. Such a testimonial is practical because the whole measure of our lives is determined from this standpoint. This means that we must live for what is lasting . . . Faith has as its goal. . .that there be an interchange of life, that Christ's life and ours be intertwined, that our lives be inscribed in his and his in ours, that the promise be fulfilled that St. Teresa of Avila heard addressed to her by the Lord: "Do not be troubled; my concerns are yours and your concerns are mine." We should live in such a way that this interchange of lives becomes a reality, that his concerns truly do become ours and ours become his, and that Christ's life and ours become inseparable.

- Pope Benedict XVI

Being holy means living exactly as our Father in heaven wants us to live. You will say that it is difficult. It is. The ideal is a very high one. And yet it is also easy. It is within our reach. When a person becomes ill, there may be no appropriate medicine. But in supernatural affairs, it is not like that. The medicine is always at hand. It is Jesus Christ, present in the Holy Eucharist, and he also gives us his grace in the other sacraments which he has established. Let us say again, in word and in action: "Lord, I trust in you; your ordinary providence, your help each day, is all I need." We do not have to ask God to perform great miracles. Rather, we have to beg him to increase our faith, to enlighten our intellect, and strengthen our will.

- St. Josemariá Escrivá

If people knew the meaning of eternity, they would be willing to do anything to amend their lives.

- Blessed Jacinta Marto

May 14

Holiness is for us of an essentially supernatural order, and God is its source. The more our souls, by means of mortification, free themselves from sin and are detached from self and creatures, the more the divine action is powerful within us. Christ tells us so. He even tells us that his Father makes use of suffering to render the life of the soul more fruitful. *I am the Vine, and my Father is the husbandman. You are the branches. Every branch that bears fruit, my Father will prune that it may bring forth more fruit.* When the eternal Father sees that a soul desires to give itself fully to Christ . . . he prunes away all that could prevent the life of Christ from producing its full effects. By the repeated and deep sufferings he permits or sends, by humiliations and contradictions, God purifies us, detaches us from creatures and empties us of self.

- Blessed Columba Marmion

Our journey through life is an interior one, a spiritual one, in which we never stay on the same plateau. We either progress or regress . . . We are all auditioning for an everlasting role in heaven. God is the auditioner; Our Lady is our constant, faithful coach. *Do whatever he tells you* were her words of advice at Cana. *Penance, penance, penance,* were her words at Lourdes in February 1858. *I have come to warn the faithful to amend their lives and ask pardon for their sins. They must not continue to offend Our Lord, who is already deeply offended,* at Fatima in October of 1917. To pass the test we have to comply with the requests of our Lady - which is conformity to the will of God.

- Louis Kaczmarek

Always walk in the presence of God because his shade is healthier than the rays of the sun. There is nothing wrong in trembling before the face of him whose very presence makes the angels tremble as they contemplate the Supreme Majesty.

- St. Francis de Sales

I see that we have to take many steps before arriving at sanctity. We think every step we take can be the last, and then we find that we have done nothing, we have hardly begun . . . A man who enters religion thinks there is nothing left to be done, but he soon finds that he has taken himself with him and is still worldly even though he has left the world . . . That done, he must go a step further and detach himself from himself, seek only God in God, and not look for any passing gain in holiness . . . to seek nothing but God's interests. For this, my Lord, you must give us a great grace, for how can we reach such purity of intention by ourselves?

- St Claude de la Colombiere

If only we could be what we hope to be, by the great kindness of our generous God. He asks so little and gives so much, in this life and in the next, to those who love him sincerely. In a spirit of hope and out of love for him, let us then bear and endure all things and give thanks for everything that befalls us.

- St. Gregory Nazianzen

The only happiness we have on earth is in loving God and in knowing that God loves us.

- St. John Vianney

The poor will be first in the kingdom of God, and the society born of Christ will not be founded on pomp, power or trust in material goods, but rather on the emptiness of this world . . . Poverty of spirit is a difficult virtue to practice today because riches - to be attained, conserved, increased, and enjoyed - have invaded the human heart . . . Christians, do not believe that you have ever done enough. Do not ever say no to the voice that begs on behalf of the poor . . . For the poor, therefore, we should have a special reverence and a great concern. They are the mirror of Christ, as it were a living sacrament of him.

- Pope Paul VI

Jesus, friend of a lonely heart, you are my haven, you are my peace. You are my salvation. You are my serenity in moments of struggle and amidst an ocean of doubts. You are the bright ray that lights up the path of my life. You are everything to a lonely soul. You understand the soul even though it remains silent. You know our weaknesses, and like a good physician, you comfort and heal, sparing us sufferings. Amen

- St. Maria Faustina Kowalska

G od alone is God, and it is he who attains all things from first to last. His grace is sovereign. His word is a keen sword. He disposes of men and moments as it pleases him. On the road to Damascus he struck down Saul, transforming him thereby into the apostle of the Gentiles. His grace is free as he is and the Spirit *blows where it wills.* He refuses to let himself be confined by us and, if it seems good to him, ignores our schemes and the limits we contrive. *My thoughts are not your thoughts and my ways are not your ways.* It is important to know this from our own experience . . . God leads and only God knows the way. God wishes to find in us docile, tractable souls through whom he can work. That is the immutable truth. It behooves us never to forget it in practice.

- Cardinal Leo Joseph Suenens

Blessed are those who for love of the Lord plunge headlong into trials and troubles without anger or sadness; when they escape, they soon reach safety in the harbor of the divinity, and through their good works come to God's home and have rest from their troubles, rejoicing in their hope. Those who run the race of life in hope, are not frightened by the trials on the way . . . On reaching the end of their course they see the Lord, and praise him for having saved them from perdition.

- John Moschus

O Jesus, why do we, such finite beings, divide ourselves into so many parts and give you so little. Why does everyone have a part of us except you? Why do we lose our way on the thorns and stones of our path? Illuminate our senses, Lord. Show us that we are nothing if not yours; that we are slaves of everything and everyone if we do not find our freedom in you; that our life is a death endured day by day if it isn't alive with your life. O Lord, dispel our darkness, our cowardice, our hesitations. The half-spent fires of love that burn with our worldly desires make more smoke and darkness than flames and light. Break into the prison that we have raised for ourselves. Come and free us and make us completely yours.

- Father Giuseppe De Luca

In heaven, everything will be spring as far as beauty is concerned, autumn as far as enjoyment is concerned, summer as far as love is concerned. There will be no winter; but here winter is necessary to exercise self-denial and a thousand other little but beautiful virtues which are exercised at times of sterility.

- St. Pio of Pietrelcina

You must ask for God's help. Even when you have done so, it may seem to you for a long time that no help, or less help than you need, is being given. Never mind. After each failure, ask forgiveness, pick yourself up and try again. Very often what God first helps us toward is not the virtue itself but just this power of always trying again. For however important chastity, or courage, or truthfulness, or any other virtue may be, this process trains us in habits of the soul which are more important still. It cures our illusions about ourselves and teaches us to depend on God. We learn, on the one hand, that we cannot trust ourselves even in our best moments, and, on the other, that we need not despair even in our worst, for our failures are forgiven.

- C. S. Lewis

L et us then leave the world, manifold and various as it is; let us leave it to follow its own devices, and let us turn to the living and true God, who has revealed himself to us in Jesus Christ. Let us be sure that he is more true than the whole world, though with one voice all its inhabitants were to speak against him. And if we doubt where the truth lies, let us pray to him to reveal it to us; let us pray him to give us humility, that we may seek aright; honesty, that we may have no concealed aims; love, that we may desire the truth; and faith, that we may accept it . . . Let us put off all excuses, all unfairness and insincerity, all trifling with our consciences, all self-deception, all delay of repentance. Let us be filled with one wish - to please God; and if we have this, I say it confidently, we shall no longer be deceived by this world. . .

- Blessed John Henry Newman

H umility is the ointment for all of our wounds.

- St. Teresa of Avila

We should desire to feel always, if we can, the effects that the presence of God produces in the soul. We should desire to contemplate him always with reverence, and to feel the sweetness of his love in the admirable intimacy of his presence. This should be our life; this is the experience that we should strive to have according to the measure of his grace in whom all grace resides, and who gives to some more, to others less. For he makes his presence felt in various ways, as he chooses. And to the possession of this gift we ought to consecrate all our lives and all our activities; without it we do not truly live, for as the soul is the life of the body, God is the life of the soul by his gracious presence.

- Father Walter Hilton

Have you forgotten that Jesus said: *It is not the healthy who need the physician, but those who are sick.* He is our Physician, and he heals our selfishness, if we let his grace penetrate to the depths of our soul. Jesus has taught us that the worst sickness is hypocrisy, the pride that leads us to hide our own sins. We have to be totally sincere with him. We have to tell the whole truth, and then we have to say: Lord, if you want to - and you always want to - you can cure me. You know my weaknesses. I feel these symptoms; I suffer from these failings. We show him the wound, with simplicity . . . Lord, you have cured so many souls; help me to recognize you as the Divine Physician, when I have you in my heart or when I contemplate your presence in the tabernacle.

- St. Josemariá Escrivá

The darkness is still with us, O Lord. You are still hidden and the world which you have made does not want to know you or receive you . . . You are still obscured by the veils of this world's history, you are still destined not to be acknowledged in the scandal of your death on the cross . . . But I, O hidden Lord of all things, boldly affirm my faith in you. In confessing you, I take my stand with you. . . If I make this avowal of faith, it must pierce the depths of my heart like a sword, I must bend my knee before you, saying, "I must alter my life."

- Karl Rahner

I can do nothing alone; my own will, however hard I exert it, does not suffice; my own plans, however astutely and systematically devised, all fail. So, there is nothing for me to do but to hand myself over to God, truly and wholly, so that he may use, or for that matter, in his wisdom not use, whatever capacity I possess to serve him.

- St. Francis de Sales

Wisdom tells us what we cannot know. Wisdom defines the limits of knowledge. Wisdom, however, always points us to a place and a purpose beyond knowledge. Wisdom takes us where knowledge can't go - to the thoughts of God and the mind of God. The summit of knowledge is to know God's will. That is the only knowledge we really need. The only knowing that is ultimately worthwhile is to know what God wants in our lives. What God always wants for us is love and the fruits of love . . . Wisdom allows us to know God, as God truly is, the "self" of God, the heart of God, the mind of God. In our world, knowledge is power. We are obsessed with power. Followers of Jesus must be different. We must be obsessed with wisdom.

- Father Harry Cronin, S.C.S.

Whatever you possess must not possess you; whatever you own must be under the power of your soul; for if your soul is overpowered by the love of this world's goods, it will be totally at the mercy of its possessions. In other words, we make use of temporal things, but our hearts are set on what is eternal. Temporal goods help us on our way, but our desire must be for those eternal realities which are our goal. We should give no more than a side glance at all that happens in the world, but the eyes of our soul are to be focused straight ahead . . . If the object of love is what is good, then the soul should take its delight in the higher good, the things of heaven. In this way, if the soul sees that we should have a greater love and a greater fear about what concerns the next life, it will never cling to this life.

- St. Gregory the Great

Let us adore Jesus in our hearts - who spent thirty years out of thirty-three in silence; who began his public life by spending forty days in silence; who often returned alone to spend the night on a mountain in silence. He who spoke with authority, now spends his earthly life in silence. Let us adore Jesus in the Eucharistic silence.

- Mother Teresa of Calcutta

God is ready to shed his graces upon us as abundantly and as usefully as those he shed upon the first Christians. He does not love us less than he loved them. All the means of sanctification that they had, we too possess; and we have besides, the examples of the saints who have followed Christ to encourage us. But we are too often like Naaman the leper who came to consult the prophet and beg his cure; he was on the point of not obtaining it because he found the remedy too simple. That is the case with some of those who undertake the spiritual life; who are so attached to their own way of seeing things that they are scandalized at the simplicity of the divine plan. And this scandal is not without harm . . . Why is this? Because all that our human ingenuity is able to create for our inner life serves for nothing if we do not base our edifice upon Christ.

- Blessed Columba Marmion

We have a God who is infinitely gracious and knows all our wants. I always thought that he would reduce you to extremity. He will come in his own time, and when you least expect it. Hope in him more than ever; thank him with me for the favors he does you . . . I do not advise you to use a multiplicity of words in prayer; many words and long discourses being often the occasions of wandering. Hold yourself in prayer before God like a poor, paralytic beggar at a rich man's gate. Let it be your business to keep your mind in the presence of the Lord . . . One way to recall the mind easily in the time of prayer, and preserve it more in tranquility, is not to let it wander too far at other times. You should keep it strictly in the presence of God.

- Brother Lawrence of the Resurrection

The book of John tells us that Jesus was tired after his journey and sat down by the well. Jesus' thirst reveals the thirst God has for us. Because God thirsts for us, he sent his beloved Son to look for us. Jesus goes wherever thirsty people can be found and invites them to drink deeply from springs of water that will never run dry. He offers us water that will bubble up within us when life stresses and leaves us parched. The request that Jesus made of the Samaritan woman: _Give me a drink_ (John 4:7), he makes of us today. This request expresses the passion of God for every human being. God wishes to awaken in each human heart, the desire for the gift of a _spring of water within, welling up for eternal life._ This is the gift of the Holy Spirit, who transforms us into true worshipers, capable of praying to the Father in spirit and truth. Only this water is capable of satisfying our thirst for goodness, truth and beauty. Only this water can irrigate the desert of our restless and parched soul, until it finds rest in God.

- Father Jerome Machar, O.C.S.O.

One could say that prayer begins here in this responsiveness to the gaze of God. Although we must make many about faces day after day to meet his gaze and to flee the oblivion to which we are so prone, every step toward purity of thought, intention, heart, toward purity of the inner eye, leads us more surely to that sanctuary called memory, a sanctuary created in us by God precisely so that we could meet him there . . . What is it to remember God? To remember him is not simply a recollection of him in his past deeds, because those mercies shape us to this day. To remember him is to enter into his presence in the varied ways that he makes himself present within and among us. It is to know that forgetfulness of God is death: *In death there is no remembrance of you* (Psalm 6:5). It is to say to God what he says to us: *I will never forget you* (Isaiah 49:15).

- Sister Maureen McCabe, O.C.S.O.

The saints already with Christ. . .have passed from a state of corruptibility to one of incorruptibility; they have gone from this world and risen again in Christ, exchanging their tent-dwelling for the heavenly Jerusalem. Leaving to us the emptiness of this life, they have attained to the bliss of heaven; leaving to us our earthly worries, they have passed to a land without worry. They have left behind the winds and waves of this world and have anchored in harbors of perfect calm. Yet even while they seemed to be with us, they were not so in reality, for their minds were turned to God. They lived on earth as citizens of heaven. Having here no lasting city, they sought a heavenly one; having no earthly riches, they sought the riches of heaven. They were strangers and sojourners as their ancestors were. Strangers to the world, to the things of the world, and to the ways of the world, their whole heart was absorbed in the things of heaven; these were the things they thought about and were concerned about . . . The saints contemplated, sought, and hastened toward these things, and so at last they attained them.

- St. Anastasius of Sinai

The little way is only for the very small. It is not for those who draw their support from their own strength, but for those who draw support from the strength of the Lord. The road is short because it is a straight road. Do not let a single chance go by for a small sacrifice, not a glance, nor a word - to take advantage of all the little things and to do them out of love.

- St. Therese of Lisieux

Life without God is nothing but death, many times over.

- St. Teresa of Avila

The Lord said, *You have not chosen me, but I have chosen you and appointed you to go and bring forth fruit* . . . Then he adds the quality the fruit is to have - *And your fruit is to endure.* Everything we labor for in this present world scarcely lasts until death. Death intervenes and cuts off the fruit of our labor. But what we do for eternal life remains even after death; it begins to appear only when the fruits of our physical labors cease to be visible . . . Let one who recognizes that he now bears eternal fruit within his soul, think little of the temporal fruits of his labors. Let us work for the fruit that endures. Let us work for the fruit that begins at death since death destroys all others.

- St. Gregory the Great

Dear Lord, help me to remove from my mind every thought or opinion which you would not sanction; every feeling from my heart which you would not approve. Grant that I may spend the hours of the day gladly working with you according to your will. Help me just for today and be with me in it: in the long hours of work, that I many not grow weary or slack in serving you; in conversations, that they may not be to me occasions of uncharitableness; in the day's worries and disappointments, that I may be patient with myself and with those around me; in the moments of fatigue and illness, that I may be mindful of others rather than of myself; in temptations, that I may be loyal; so that when the day is over I may lay it at your feet, with its successes which are all yours, and its failures which are all my own, and feel that life is real and peaceful and blessed when spent with you as the guest of my soul. Amen

Solitude is not a solution but a direction. The echo of this direction is heard in the prophet Elijah, who did not find Yahweh in the mighty wind, or the earthquake, or the fire, but in the still, small voice . . . Every time we enter into solitude, we withdraw from our windy, tornado-like, fiery lives and we open ourselves for the great encounter, the meeting with Love. But first in our solitude is the discovery of our own restlessness, our drivenness, our compulsiveness, our urge to act quickly, to make an impact, and to have influence . . . But when we persevere with the help of a gentle discipline, we slowly come to hear the still, small voice and to feel the delicate breeze, and so come to know the presence of Love. This Love goes straight to the heart, making us see the truth of who we really are. We are God's beloved children.

- Henri Nouwen

The Sermon on the Mount is about being fully alive in Jesus Christ. It is about nourishing the eternal life within us. The Sermon on the Mount is demanding. It is just not enough to avoid external sins of great magnitude. We have to fight . . . our anger, our hatred, our grudges, our past hurts. Hatred, anger, and grudges destroy the life of Christ within us. We have to teach our children that there is never room for hatred in the world. If we allow what upsets us to turn into hatred, we destroy ourselves, we destroy our ability to live genuine lives, the life of Jesus within us. We cannot love God and hate another person at the same time. St. Leo the Great used to challenge the Christians of the fifth century by saying "Remember your dignity." We also have to remember the dignity we have, the dignity of being fully alive with the life of Jesus Christ.

- Father Joseph Pellegrino

We have to hang on to the fact of God's love for us. That demands courage and tenacity. There is so much in the world that seems to contradict the whole idea . . . there is enough in our own lives to make us doubt it. No one has ever given a totally satisfactory explanation of why there is evil and so much suffering in life . . . But there are truths which point us in the right direction . . . There is the fact that God became man, accepted the human condition and gave it a new significance and value. We have to hang on all the time to the fact that God loves us, and this in every crisis and however much events and facts appear to contradict the truth. We must trust God . . . God asks us, sometimes often, to go on with the pilgrimage through life in the dark, but always trusting. Trust is a proof of love.

- Cardinal Basil Hume

We need the greater and lesser hopes that keep us going day by day. But these are not enough without the great hope, which must surpass everything else. This great hope can only be God, who encompasses the whole of reality and who can bestow upon us what we, by ourselves, cannot attain . . . God is the foundation of hope. Not any god, but the God who has a human face and who has loved us to the end, each one of us and humanity in its entirety. His kingdom is not an imaginary hereafter, situated in a future that will never arrive; his kingdom is present wherever he is loved and wherever his love reaches us. His love alone gives us the possibility of soberly persevering day by day, without ceasing to be spurred on by hope, in a world which by its very nature is imperfect. His love is at the same time our guarantee of the existence of what we only vaguely sense and which nevertheless, in our deepest self, we await: a life that is "truly life."

- Pope Benedict XVI

Knowing that God loves us is happiness . . . They, the Father, Son and Holy Spirit, will come to us, *and they will make their home with us.* They will keep us company. This is Christ's own definition of happiness - the awareness of God being at home in our souls. Yes, there are two homes in which the Trinity dwells, one in heaven with the angels and saints and the other on earth in the hearts of those who are doing God's will . . . What then, does it mean to be truly happy? It means to experience the presence of God, whether by faith and imperfectly in this life, or by vision and without end in the life to come.

- Father John Hardon

When we lose touch with the eternal truths, we get submerged in the weeds that sprout all over the garden of our life. They are senseless trivialities that assume an air of real importance. Though they pretend to have a purpose, they are quite futile, and merely add obscurity and confusion to a life which is gradually engulfed in a sort of eternal twilight without light or direction . . . It is hard enough to meet the ordinary hazards incidental to every existence; but the Godless person has no defenses and is delivered up, bound and disarmed . . . There is only one remedy for such a state; each person must return to God, listen to his inner voice, and consciously make contact with him.

- Father Alfred Delp, S.J.

When you give, give generously, your face lit up with joy. And give more than you were asked for . . . Make no distinction between rich and poor. Do not try to find out who is worthy and who is not. Let all people be equal in your eyes . . . The Lord ate at the table of the tax collectors and sinners. He did not keep the unworthy at a distance. He wanted thus to draw all humankind to himself. Therefore consider that all human beings . . . are equal in worth and honor, and that each one of them, in virtue of his nature, is your brother.

- Isaac of Nineveh

Whatever be my age, whatever the number of my years, I am ever narrowing the interval between time and eternity. I am ever changing in myself . . . I know O my God, I must change, if I am to see thy face. I must undergo the change of death. Body and soul must die to this world. My real self, my soul, must change by a true regeneration. Let me day by day be molded upon thee, and be changed from glory to glory, by ever looking toward thee, and ever leaning on thy arm . . . I know not what lies before me but I know as much as this. I know, too, that if thou art not with me, my change will be for the worse, not for the better. All will turn to good if I have Jesus with me, yesterday and today the same, and forever.

- Blessed John Henry Newman

L ittle we are, before the task we have to accomplish, as I have now tried to make you see in the light of Love's demands . . . But none of this can be real and genuine unless our hearts are changed and become humble, freed of self-love, surrendered beyond question to the love of Jesus Crucified. And that is the work of a lifetime, a work to be begun again each morning. To find Jesus, to love Jesus, to live for Jesus; to be literally and unremittingly possessed by a great desire to love each and every person with true devotion . . . to be eager to be little and nothing but a poor worker on earth - that, Little Brothers of Jesus, is what your name means. That, too, is what you must strive to bring about in your lives by handing them over, in humble, confident self- abandonment, to the action of the Spirit of Love.

- Father Rene Voillaume

Lord, you know that you alone are the life of my soul, my highest love, my light, my God, my all. Without you life is so dead, so empty. Without you, Lord, life is not worth living.

- Blessed Pauline von Mallinekrodt

We believe that doing little things for God is as much a way of loving him as doing great deeds. Besides, we are not very well informed about the greatness of our acts. There are nevertheless two things we know for sure: first, whatever we do can't help but be small; and second, whatever God does is great. And so we go about our activities with a sense of great peace. We know that all our work consists in not shifting about under grace; in not choosing what we would do; and that it is God who acts through us. There is nothing difficult for God; the one who grows anxious at difficulties is the one who counts on his own capacity for action . . . Our feet march upon a street, but our heartbeat reverberates through the whole world. That is why our small acts . . . perfectly join together the love of God and the love of our neighbor . . . And thus life becomes a celebration.

- Madeleine Delbrel

L et us think often that our only business in this life is to please God, and that all besides is but folly and vanity. You and I have lived in monastic life more than forty years. Have we employed those years in loving and serving God, who by his mercy has called us to this state, and for that very end? . . . Since by his mercy he gives us still a little time, let us begin in earnest; let us repair the lost time; let us return with a wholehearted trust to that Father of mercies, who is always ready to receive us into his loving arms. Let us renounce and renounce generously, with single heart, for the love of him, all that is not he; he deserves infinitely more. Let us think of him perpetually. Let us put all our trust in him.

- Brother Lawrence of the Resurrection

The person who has honestly resolved to seek the love of God may be said already to possess that love in his or her heart. For that resolution is a proof that the grace of God has descended into the depths of the person's heart, to kindle there a longing for God's love. What we must do is set no obstacle to the growth of this love within us, so that it may pervade our whole being more and more. We must ask God, the object of our love, to give us the sweetly compelling power of divine grace, to reach into the depths of our soul and set a spring of love there so that its waters may make fertile the dry and barren places of our lovelessness.

- Karl Rahner

Your great intention in receiving Communion should be to advance, strengthen, and comfort yourself in the love of God. If worldly people ask you why you receive Communion so often, tell them that it is to learn to love God, to be purified from your imperfections, delivered from misery, comforted in affliction, and supported in weakness.

- St. Francis de Sales

Whenever things go monstrously wrong, the first casualty is always hope. It is fragile, like rare cut glass. We can lose it so easily. St. Paul tells us that, for those who follow Christ, there is Someone who protects and saves our hope; the Father of Jesus. St. Paul tells us that our hope is safe with God. It is well beyond any damage that can be afflicted by human disaster or natural cataclysm. God truly holds our hope and guards it.

- Father Harry Cronin, C.S.C.

We need silence. We need to be alone or together looking for God in silence. There it is that we accumulate the inward power by which we act, by which we do the smallest duty and by which we suffer the severest hardships that befall us . . . Once I was asked by someone what I consider the most important aspect of the training of the Sisters of our Order. I answered, "Silence," - interior and exterior silence. Silence is essential in a religious house. The silence of humility, of charity, the silence of the eyes, of the ears, of the tongue. There is no life of prayer without silence. Silence, and then kindness, charity; silence leads to charity, and charity to humility.

- Mother Teresa of Calcutta

We should attach no importance either to the events of this life or to material things; they are the dreams of a night spent at an inn, and will vanish as quickly as images seen in dreams, leaving no more traces than they do . . . We must see things as they are, in the great light of the faith which illumines our thoughts with daylight so bright that we see things with an eye very different from that of poor souls tied to the world. Like faith itself, the habit of seeing things in the light of faith raises us above the mists and mud of this world. At every moment of our lives, in time and in eternity, we must live by faith, believing in what grace leads us to hope for, expecting to possess it in glory, loving him who will be "our infinite reward."

- Blessed Charles de Foucauld

To suffer-what does it signify? It is only for a moment. If we could go and pass a week in heaven, we should understand the value of this moment of suffering . . . The Cross is the gift that God makes to his friends. How beautiful it is to offer ourselves every morning in sacrifice to the good God, and to accept everything in expiation for our sins. We must ask for the love of crosses; then they become sweet. I did this for four or five years. I was greatly calumniated, greatly contradicted, greatly knocked about. Oh, I had crosses indeed! I had almost more than I could carry. Then I took to asking for love of crosses, and I was happy . . . We must not wonder where our crosses come from. They come from God. It is always God who gives us this way of proving our love to him.

- St. John Vianney

Christ said that it was difficult for "the rich" to enter the kingdom of heaven, referring no doubt, to "riches" in the ordinary sense. But I think it really covers riches in every sense - good fortune, health, popularity, and all the things one wants to have. All these things tend - just as money tends - to make you feel independent of God, because if you have them, you are happy already and contented in this life.

- C. S. Lewis

Humility is perpetual quietness of heart. It is to have no trouble. It is never to be fretted, or vexed, or irritated, or disappointed. It is to expect nothing, to wonder at nothing that is done to me, to feel nothing done against me. It is to be at rest when nobody praises me. And when I am blamed and despised, it is to have a blessed home within myself, where I can go in and shut the door, and kneel to my Heavenly Father in secret, and be at peace, as in a deep sea of calmness, when all around and above is trouble.

– Canon Thomas Carter

J esus showed me a robe which he called, "the robe of innocence." It was whiter than snow. He put it on me saying, "With this, I am taking from you forever all ill will.". . .Then, opening to me his adorable Heart and putting me within it, he said, "This will be the place of your present and continual dwelling." Since then I have always seen and found myself in this lovable Heart in a way I do not know how to explain, unless by saying that sometimes it was as though I were in a beautiful garden with flowers growing all around; at other times like a minnow in a vast ocean, or like gold being purified in a crucible. But usually it is like a furnace of pure love.

- St. Margaret Mary Alacoque

God manifests himself in his Son and becomes for me the Way. . .I am alive only if I give my will over to the will of God. Only in this way does conversion become true; only in this way does the remembrance of God arrive in me and create life for me. . .He has to enter into the depth of our feelings, of our emotional, preconscious decisions and make himself present there, for they can be the lead weight that drags us down, but they can also become the wings by which we can reach the heights and the open air . . . He has touched not only our understanding but our hearts. He has shown that he is kind. Only when we begin to love God, that is, only when we begin to recognize that the truth is worth living, that the Commandments are not an external imposition but rather, are in the service of love, only when we learn to see this in Christ does our will become free; only then do we become converts; then life really begins in us. Let us ask the Lord to allow this to happen to us . . . Let us ask him to grant us real conversion, day by day, so that we might learn to live. Amen.

- Pope Benedict XVI

O Lord, your love is a gift that is more precious than gold. From the beginning of creation your Son, the eternal Word, has been tossing about on the stormy waters of human souls, striving to bring peace through the gift of love. Now he has breathed over the waters of our souls, and the waves are calm. Merciful Father, we thank you.

- William of St. Thierry

The Holy Spirit did not descend just once, a long time ago, upon the apostles; he still wants to shed his burning effusion in the soul of each one of us. If we could be positively certain of the intimacy that God wishes to have with us, how happy we would be! Everything would then have a meaning . . . Things which we still regard as too painful would no longer be so, if we could recognize the Divine Guest who has made his abode in us. Instead of turning hither and yon, seeking in things and people, a firm support which we ought not to ask of them, why don't we wait for the coming of the incomparable Friend that God wishes to be to us? Perhaps we might try to make up, right now, for the too-slight desire men have for God, by longing greatly for the coming of the Holy Spirit.

- Mother Marie Des Douleurs

It is only when God withdraws his help and leaves the proud man to his own devices, that it becomes evident what a man is worth without God . . . Humility is a supernatural virtue by which we lovingly recognize our true value in God's eyes, and are disposed to render him due recognition for all the good we find in ourselves . . . We are the soil in which Christ grows; his roots will only pick out from us what is in accordance with his Father's will - and therefore it depends upon us to decide whether by doing the will of God we are to be absorbed by Christ and are to enter into life - or to be left by him in the exterior darkness of our own will.

- Father Eugene Boylan, O.C.S.O.

How should we regard life as we go through it? We are immortal: independent of time and space. This life is but a sort of outward stage on which we act for a time. We should consider ourselves to be in this world as players are in a game; and this life is as different from our real existence as a dream differs from waking. And yet it is a serious dream as we are judged by our actions. And so the spiritual man goes through life doing his actions for God's sake. It is this view of life that removes from us all surprise and disappointment that this life is so incomplete . . . The one desire which should move us all is the desire to see God face to face.

- Blessed John Henry Newman

O my God, Trinity whom I adore, help me to forget myself entirely that I may be established in you as still and as peaceful as if my soul were already in eternity. May nothing trouble my peace or make me leave you, O my unchanging One, but may each minute carry me further into the depths of your mystery. Give peace to my soul; make it your heaven, your beloved dwelling place. May I never leave you there alone but be wholly present, my faith wholly vigilant, wholly adoring, and wholly surrendered to your creative action.

- St. Elizabeth of the Trinity

Be kind to your little children, Lord. Be a gentle teacher, patient with our weakness. Give us the strength and discernment to do what you tell us and so to grow in your likeness. May we all live in the peace that comes from you. May we journey toward your city, sailing through the waters, untouched by the waves of sin, borne serenely along by the Holy Spirit. Night and day may we give you praise and thanks, because you have shown us that all things belong to you and all blessings are gifts from you. To you, the essence of wisdom, the foundation of truth, be glory for evermore.

- St. Clement of Alexandria

Lord, grant me the grace to sever all the ties that bind me to this earth, to renounce all worldly trifles, to free myself from all kinds of worldly desires, appetites, pursuits, and plans so that I may boldly say - I no longer fear anyone on earth. I only fear you, my Lord, my God and Creator. I fear only that I may please you less than I am able, that I may do less for your glory than my powers, aided by your grace, can perform.

- Blessed George Matulaitis

This hidden God who challenges our faith, teaches us at the same time, by his example. He gives himself, unresisting, into our hands; we are to give ourselves unresisting into his hands, without struggle, without reservations, without misgiving. The inner reality of our souls is to be something different from anything the world sees. Behind the mask of our daily cares and preoccupations, there is to be some other foundation for our lives, a continual aspiration toward God and a desire for his presence.

- Monsignor Ronald Knox

God knows best what is needful for us, and all that he does is for our good. If we knew how much he loves us, we should always be ready to receive equally and with indifference from his hand, the sweet as well as the bitter. All would please that came from him. The sorest afflictions never appear intolerable except when we see them in the wrong light. When we see them dispensed by the hand of God, when we know that it is our loving Father who abases and distresses us, our sufferings lose all their bitterness and our mourning becomes all joy.

- Brother Lawrence of the Resurrection

It is not new to fall; what is wrong is to lie down after you have fallen. Remember where you stood before you fell. The devil once mocked you, but now he will know that you can rise stronger than ever before . . . Do not draw back from the mercy of God.

- St. Abraham Kidunaia

Dear Lord, free me from my dark past, into which I often find myself falling as if into a deep cistern. . .Keep showing me your light, and give me the strength to rise and follow you without ever looking back.

- Henri Nouwen

Trials are not only good for us, but necessary for our spiritual growth, especially if endured with the right disposition. During hard times, God helps us see that control is really an illusion. We're not in charge. Our lives don't even belong to us. We would cease to exist if the Holy Spirit stopped actively sustaining our existence, even for one second . . . God is more responsible for our lives than we are. Our job is to listen, humble ourselves, work hard and not get in his way.

- Anonymous

Our wound is serious, but the Physician is all-powerful. Does it seem to you so small a mercy that, while you were living in evil and sinning, He did not take away your life, but brought you to belief and forgave your sins? What I suffer is serious, but I trust the Almighty. I would despair of my mortal wound if I had not found so great a Physician.

- St. Augustine

Private time spent in the presence of the Blessed Sacrament is one of the most effective ways of drawing closer to Jesus. The world is filled with noise. We all need quiet time to gather our thoughts, to speak to God and to listen to him. If we can do this in the presence of the Blessed Sacrament, we are very fortunate. . . Jesus is present in the Most Blessed Sacrament to complete the work which his Father entrusts to him. He is there to fill our soul with the love which led him to die on the Cross for us . . . Jesus gave his all for us. We should be giving more of ourselves to him.

- Bishop Thomas V. Daily

Oh God, infinite holiness, goodness and perfection, lead me to sanctity. Increase and refine my love. Turn it into a burning flame, a fiery furnace of love. Raise me above my mundane self. Do for me what I am unable to do for myself. Drown my pride, my selfishness and attachments in the abyss of the love and humility of thy Sacred Heart.

- Louis Kaczmarek

For most people, daily life in the secular world is the place where transformation in Christ is worked out. Like the Pharisee in the scriptures, one can be in religious life and not be transformed. So what is it that makes the difference? . . . It is the hidden action of the kingdom of God that works, not so much through external circumstances, as through a radical change in our attitudes. This is what transformation is. The ordinary circumstances of daily life bring back the same faults, the same temptations, the same routines, and often the sense of going nowhere. But "nowhere" is where the kingdom of God is most active. Grace and daily life are always in dialogue. . .

- Father Thomas Keating, O.C.S.O.

How devout you and I should be, my dear brother, in order to thank Our Lord and the most Holy Virgin for the signal grace of having called us to his service, we who are so weak and so ignorant. Let us apply ourselves to studying the saints by imitating their virtues of humility, obedience, charity and self-denial. Let us often remember the words of the divine Master, who tells us, *I have come not to be served, but to serve.* That seems difficult to our nature, but when we love Our Lord, everything becomes easy. When it is difficult for us, let us immediately say, "Everything to please you, O My God, and nothing to please me." Another thought that has done me great good is, "Always do what costs us the most."

- St. Bernadette Soubirous

Let us imagine that we are a brush in the hand of an infinitely perfect artist. What must a brush do to make the painting turn out most beautiful? It must allow itself to be guided as perfectly as possible . . . When Eternal Wisdom, God, uses us as an instrument, then we shall act most fruitfully . . . when we permit ourselves to be directed most perfectly and entirely.

- St. Maximilian Maria Kolbe

In order to enter the fullness of the hidden life, it is not enough to hide oneself from the attention of others; we must also hide from ourselves, that is, forget ourselves, avoiding all excessive concern about ourselves ... To be overly concerned about one's spiritual progress, about the consolations which God gives or does not give, about the state of aridity in which one may be - all this is often the sign of a subtle spiritual egoism, a sign that the soul is more occupied with itself than with God. We must learn to forget ourselves, to hide from ourselves, by refusing to examine too minutely what is happening within our soul and by not attaching too much importance to it.

- Father Gabriel of St. Mary Magdalene

Let us not lament if we suffer from some natural defect of body or mind; from poor memory, slowness of understanding, little ability . . . or general bad health. What claim have we, or what obligation is God under, to give us a more brilliant mind or a more robust body? Who is ever offered a gift and then lays down the conditions upon which he will accept it? Who knows? Perhaps if God had given us greater talent, better health, a more personable appearance, we might have lost our souls. Great talent and knowledge have caused many to be puffed up with the idea of their own importance . . . How many, on the contrary, who, by reason of poverty, infirmity or physical deformity, have become saints and have saved their souls . . . But one thing is necessary and it is not beauty, not health, not talent. It is the salvation of our immortal souls.

- St. Alphonsus Liguori

You are one of God's people, of God's family . . . When you are in your room then, at night, think always on Christ, and wait for his coming at every moment. This is the person Christ has loved in loving you, the person he has chosen in choosing you. He enters by the open door; he has promised to come in, and he cannot deceive. Embrace him, the one you have sought; turn to him and be enlightened; hold him fast, ask him not to go in haste, beg him not to leave you. The word of God moves swiftly; he is not won by the lukewarm, nor held fast by the negligent. Let your soul be attentive to his word; follow carefully the path God tells you to take, for he is swift in his passing. Whoever seeks Christ in this way, whoever prays to Christ in this way, is not abandoned by him; on the contrary, Christ comes again and again to visit such a person, for he is with us until the end of the world.

- St. Ambrose

In the course of this our earthly pilgrimage, the Lord leads us in his ways; either he gives us his hand to have us walk with him or he carries us in the arms of his Divine Providence. He holds us by the hand when he enables us to walk by the exercise of virtue; if he did not, we would not be able to walk at all on this blessed way. There is plenty of evidence that those who let go of his fatherly hand cannot take one step without falling and hitting the ground. Without a doubt, the good God wants to lead us, wants to help us on our way, but he also wants us to do our part by taking small steps in cooperation with his grace.

- St. Francis de Sales

Interior silence, the inner stillness to which meditation leads, is where the Spirit secretly anoints the soul and heals our deepest wounds.

- St. John of the Cross

Once the world held us by its delights. Now it is so full of disasters that the world itself is summoning us to God. Consider the emptiness of things which pass away with time. Let the end of what is temporal show that what can pass away amounts to nothing. Let the fall of things reveal their transitory nature, and that what appeared to be lasting amounts to almost nothing. Consider these things carefully, dearly beloved. Fix your hearts on love of what is eternal, so that when you decline to strive for earthly heights you may attain the glory you grasp by faith.

- St. Gregory the Great

Your losses remind you that all isn't perfect, that you had hoped that many events in your life would not have been so painful, but they were. You find yourself disillusioned with the irrevocable personal losses; your health, your spouse, your job, your hope, your dream. Your whole life is filled with losses, endless losses. And every time there are losses there are choices to be made. You choose to live your losses as passages to anger, blame, hatred, depression, and resentment, or you choose to let these losses be passages to something new, something wider, and deeper. The question is not how to avoid loss and make it not happen, but how to choose it as a passage, as an exodus to greater life and freedom.

- Henri Nouwen

We would envy our religious brothers and sisters if we too could "die to ourselves" a little more each day. However, for us, the tiny circumstances of life are faithful "superiors." They do not leave us alone for a moment. When we surrender to them without resistance, we find ourselves wonderfully liberated from ourselves. From the moment we wake up, these circumstances take hold of us. It is the telephone that rings; it is the key that won't work, the bus that doesn't arrive or arrives full . . . It's the daily routine, one chore that leads to another, some job we wouldn't have chosen. It's being cold, or being hot; it's the headache or the toothache. For us, the ordinary people of the streets, obedience means bending to the ways of our times whenever they are not harmful . . . When we live with others, obedience also means we set aside our own tastes and leave things in the place others have put them. When we thus become accustomed to giving up our will to so many tiny things, we will no longer find it hard, when the occasion presents itself, to do the will of our boss, our husband, or our parents.

- Madeleine Delbrel

I always recall that wonderful phrase of St. Paul, *This is the will of God, your sanctification . . .* It does not only mean that it is God's will we should be holy, but that our holiness will be the doing of his will. God's will is shown to us in many ways. We are born into this world, and the will of God is around us - even before our birth. We are born surrounded by the will of God and that will is now going to be our sanctification. God's will is manifested to us even by what we are ourselves. We are not angels. Had we been angels, our eternity would have been settled by one act. We are human beings with that strange wedlock between body and soul. That is the will of God. Our very body is the will of God, and our sanctification depends on our accepting the will of God with regard to our body and our soul. Do not think, dear children in Jesus Christ, do not think that it is always easy to do the will of God.

- Father Vincent McNabb, O.P.

R emember always that the Son of God remained unrecognized. That is our aim, and that is what he asks of us now, for the future, and for always, unless he shows us, by some method of his which we cannot mistake, that he wants something else of us. Pay homage to the everyday life led by our Lord on earth, to his humility, his self- surrender, and his practice of the virtues such a life requires. But chiefly pay homage to the limitations our Divine Master set on his own achievements. He did not choose to do all he might have done, and he teaches us to be content to refrain from undertakings which might be within our power, and to fulfill only what charity demands and his will requires.

- St. Vincent de Paul

We must go to God and ask him to empty us of self and of self-seeking and of self-regard. We want to consecrate to God every possession, every action, every moment we live. Let us tell God that all we have and enjoy comes from him, belongs to him, that we hold it only at his disposal. We want to refer to him credit for anything we do. We want to consecrate to him all our pleasures, offer to him all our defects and discomforts. I have nothing my God, it is all yours. Take it. I give it back to you.

- Monsignor Ronald Knox

Nothing is more essential than the love of God. It is the first of all virtues, a virtue so necessary, that without it we shall never get to heaven; and it is in order to love God that we are on the earth . . . But the misfortune is that we lavish our love upon objects unworthy of it, and refuse it to him alone who deserves to be infinitely loved. Thus my children, one person will love riches, another will love pleasures; and both will offer to the good God nothing but the languishing remains of a heart worn out in the service of the world . . . God alone . . . deserves that we should love him above all things; more than our possessions, because they are earthly; more than our friends, because they are mortal; more than our life, because it is perishable; more than ourselves, because we belong to him. Our love, my children, if it is true, must be without limit, and it must influence our conduct.

- St. John Vianney

L et us love sacrifice; let us seek atonement. How? By uniting ourselves in the Mass to Christ, who is Priest and Victim. He is always the one who bears the tremendous weight of the infidelities of men - your infidelities and mine . . . He is a teacher, with a knowledge that only he possesses - the knowledge of unlimited love for God, and, in God, for all men. In Christ's teaching, we learn that our existence does not belong to us. He gave up his life for all men and, if we follow him, we must understand that we cannot take possession of our own lives in a selfish way, without sharing the sorrows of others. Our life belongs to God. We are here to spend it in his service, concerning ourselves generously with souls, showing, through our words and our example, the extent of the Christian dedication that is expected of us.

- St. Josemariá Escrivá

You know that God is everywhere . . . that is to say, wherever God is, there is heaven . . . Remember how St. Augustine tells us about his seeking God in many places and eventually finding him within himself. Do you suppose it is of little importance that a soul which is often distracted should come to understand this truth and to find that, in order to speak to its Eternal Father and to take its delight in him, it has no need to go to heaven or speak in a loud voice? However quietly we speak, he is so near that he will hear us; we need no wings to go in search of him but have only to find a place where we can be alone and look upon him present within us . . . We must talk to him very humbly, as we should to our father, ask him for things as we should ask a father, tell him our troubles, and beg him to put them right.

- St. Teresa of Avila

You have said "yes" to Jesus and he has taken you at your word . . . God cannot fill what is already full. He can fill only emptiness, deep poverty and your "yes" is the beginning of being or becoming empty. It is not how much we have to give, but how empty we are - so that we can receive fully in our life and let him live his life in us. Take your eyes away from yourself and rejoice that you have nothing, that you are nothing, that you can do nothing. Give Jesus a big smile each time your nothingness frightens you.

- Mother Teresa of Calcutta

John Paul II's words to the world, "Do not be afraid," echo the words of Jesus. These words reveal something of the Pope's awareness of the precariousness of life and the need for a compass, which is the Lord . . . Our lives are small. It was Moses to whom God spoke, from a small wind. The wind has been silent a long time . . . The winds may seem overwhelming and beyond our control to calm them. But it is then and perhaps only then, that the wind will speak again, calming all about us, and urging us to move on and not be afraid. We will need to be still and listen - listen with the heart. The heart - a small thing. It does not occupy much space but holds something of the eternal. It guides us through what is necessarily vast and of mystery. Like a compass, it contains all directions and yet points to the One that is necessary.

- Father James Behrens, O.C.S.O.

We may make an oratory of our heart wherein to retire from time to time to converse with God in meekness, humility, and love. Every one is capable of such familiar conversation with God, some more, some less. He knows what we can do. Let us begin, then . . . Let us live and die with God. Sufferings will be sweet and pleasant to us while we are with him; and the greatest pleasures will be, without him, a cruel punishment to us. May he be blessed forever. Amen

- Brother Lawrence of the Resurrection

Three streams flow ceaselessly from Jesus' divine heart. The first is a stream of mercy for sinners, giving them a spirit of contrition and repentance. The second is a stream of charity, which brings help to all in need, especially to those who seek perfection and need help overcoming difficulties. The third is a stream of love and light, which flows into those with whom our Lord wants to share his knowledge and commandments so that they, each in their own way, may devote themselves wholly to promoting his glory.

- St. Margaret Mary Alacoque

God gave me the grace of knowing the world just enough to despise it and separate myself from it . . . I must admit this life had its charms for me . . . I consider it a great grace not to have remained in Alencon. The friends we had there were too worldly . . . They didn't think about death enough, and yet death had paid its visit to a great number of those whom I knew, the young, the rich, the happy! I love to return in spirit to the enchanting places where they lived, wondering where these people are, what became of their houses and gardens where I saw them enjoy life's luxuries. And I see that all is vanity and vexation of spirit under the sun, that the only good is to love God with all one's heart and to be poor in spirit here on earth.

- St. Therese of Lisieux

A deep peace floods the soul; transitory things are nothing. We are walking toward God, contemplating his immense happiness and rejoicing forever in the thought of the infinite, perfect, unchangeable happiness of this God we love; we are happy with the happiness of the Beloved, and the thought of his unchangeable peace calms the soul . . . The sight of my own nothingness does not weigh me down. It helps me forget myself and think only of him who is all in all.

- Blessed Charles de Foucauld

L ord, the silence in my soul is deafening. Prayers dash themselves against an impregnable wall. You dwell just beyond that wall . . . I am waiting, Lord. Waiting for your joy to uplift me. For your light to be rekindled in my dark soul. For your pervading peace. For your steadfast love. Waiting for you to possess me again. Come, dearest Lord, enfold me in your arms and abolish the pain of my separation from you.

- Virginia Ulrich

We need to know the littleness of all created beings and to set as nothing, everything that is made. We do that in order to love and possess God who is unmade. This is the reason why we do not feel complete ease in our hearts and souls. We look here for satisfaction in things which are so trivial, where there is no rest to be found. We do not know our God who is almighty, all wise, all good. He is rest itself. God wishes to be known and is pleased that we should rest in him. All that is here below does not satisfy us and this is why, until all that is made seems as nothing, no soul can be at rest. When a soul sets all at nothing for love, in order to have him who is everything, then he is able to receive spiritual rest.

- Julian of Norwich

Iwill live in the present moment and fill it with love. A straight line is made of millions of little points, one united with the other. My life, too, is made of millions of seconds and minutes united one with the other. If I arrange every single point perfectly, the line will be straight. If I live every minute perfectly, my life will be holy. The road of hope is paved with little steps of hope. The life of hope is made of brief minutes of hope . . . Every minute I want to sing with the whole Church - *Glory be to the Father and to the Son and to the Holy Spirit.*

- Father Francis Xavier Nguyen Van Thuan

We should, I believe, distrust states of mind which turn our attention upon ourselves. Even at our sins, we should look no longer than is necessary to know and to repent of them; and our virtues or progress are certainly a dangerous object of contemplation. When the sun is vertically above a man, it casts no shadow; similarly when we have come to the Divine meridian, our spiritual shadow (that is, our consciousness of self) will vanish. One will thus, in a sense, be almost nothing: a room to be filled by God and our blessed fellow creatures . . .

- C. S. Lewis

God wants our trust, and only then can he help us. To see persons open to trust is a sign of the Holy Spirit, and if our "Yes" to him is true, even when we find ourselves in situations of suffering, this will not be a suffering that damages, but one that strengthens us and transforms our tired faith into living faith. Obedience doesn't take away suffering, but gives us strength to leave all that disturbs us on the altar. Your problems remain in good hands, in the hands of God . . . Sometimes we carry heavy weights in our hearts. We have to deposit them in the heart of God.

- Sister Elvira Petrozzi

When loneliness comes upon you, when you want to go and hide in some corner, when self-pity tosses you like a huge wave on a beach full of stones and you think you are going to be broken up by them - when this happens, close your eyes and repeat, *In my heart there is a garden enclosed* (Song of Songs 4:12). The enclosure is for God and the waves have brought you into this garden, where the feelings of self-pity and anger and all kinds of reactions will disappear . . . God will enlighten you. He will give you the grace to truly believe in his love for you. God loves us so much. Are we ready to fall in love with him or are we just floating from one place to another, like a leaf falling from a tree, wafted by the wind and getting nowhere.

- Catherine de Hueck Doherty

I thank you, Lord, for all that you have asked of me in my life. Be praised for the time in which I was born, glorified for my hours of happiness and my days of misery, blessed for everything that you have denied me. Lord . . . never dismiss me from your service. You have power over my heart . . . Keep me in your service all the days of my life . . . You will give me the strength to make a fresh start again and again; to hope against hope; in all my defeats to have faith in victory and in your triumph within me.

- Karl Rahner

Let us every day do our best to advance in God, and to be sparing with the transitory possessions we are going to leave behind us in this world. Let us pay attention to Abraham's faith, because he was also our father. Let us imitate his devotion and faith. We are Christians, and strangers on earth. Let none of us be frightened; our native land is not in this world.

- St. Augustine

There is no holiness, Lord, if you withdraw your hand. No wisdom is of any use if you no longer guide it. No strength can avail if you do not preserve it. No purity is safe if you do not protect it. No watchfulness on our part can affect anything unless your holy vigilance is present with us. If you abandon us, we sink and perish; but if you come to us, we are raised up and we live.

- Thomas à Kempis

Jesus, in whom the fullness of God dwells, has become our home. By making his home in us, he allows us to make our home in him. By entering into the intimacy of our innermost self, he offers us the opportunity to enter into his own intimacy with God. By choosing us as his preferred dwelling place, he invites us to choose him as our preferred dwelling place. . . To those who are tortured by inner or outer fear, and who desperately look for the house of love where they can find the intimacy their heart's desire, Jesus says, "You have a home . . . I am your home . . . claim me as your home . . . it is right where you are . . . in your innermost being . . . in your heart." The more attentive we are to such words, the more we realize that we do not have to go far to find what we are searching for. The tragedy is that we are so possessed by fear that we do not trust our innermost self as an intimate place but anxiously wander around hoping to find it where we are not. We try to find that intimate place in knowledge, competence, notoriety, success, friends, sensations, pleasure, dreams, or artificially induced states of consciousness. Thus we become strangers to ourselves, people who have an address but are never home and hence can never be addressed by the true voice of love.

- Henri Nouwen

My God, teach me to recognize your action in everything, in every creature that hurts me, in every happening which crosses me, as much as in every joy that delights me. Give me to understand in practice that if secondary causes are infinitely varied, there is but one first cause, and that first cause is you, Lord. The hand is the same, though the glove may be changed . . . O God, my God, it is always your good and tender hand which clasps mine to tell me, "I love you."

- Cardinal Leo Joseph Suenens

I desire to love you, O my God, with a love that is patient, with a love that abandons itself wholly to you, with a love that acts, and most important of all, with a love that perseveres. Just as one who loves a creature thinks of him often, so let the lover of God have him often in his thoughts. The mirror into which we must look in order to attain divine love is Jesus Christ. If the actions of our neighbors had a hundred sides, we ought to look at them on the best side. When an action is blameworthy, we should strive to see the good intentions behind it. Let us do everything for love and, remembering that love longs for love alone, nothing can appear hard to us.

- St. Theresa Margaret of the Sacred Heart

We cannot be missionaries if we have not sincerely, generously, and warmly welcomed the word of God, the Gospel, within ourselves. The vital dynamic of this word is to take on flesh, to become flesh in us. And when this word comes to dwell within us, we become capable of being missionaries . . . Once we have heard God's word, we no longer have the right not to accept it . . . Henceforward, we belong to all those who are waiting for the word. The time of martyrs comes and goes, but the time of witnesses continues without end - and being witnesses means being martyrs. This incarnation of God's word in us, this allowing ourselves to be molded by it, is what we call witnessing. To take the word of God seriously, we need all the strength of the Holy Spirit. If our witness is often mediocre, it is because we have not realized that the same kind of heroism is needed to be a witness as to be a martyr . . . At the beginning of each hour of the long day, we could say, "I must begin this hour as if I were going to be a martyr, and a witness" - because there is not one second that we have the right to let God's word lie dormant in us.

- *Madeleine Delbrel*

Jesus is preeminently the Good Shepherd . . . Each soul can say: Jesus knows me and loves me, not in a general abstract way, but in the concrete aspect of my needs, of my desires, and of my life; for him to know me and to love me is to do me good, to encompass me more and more with his grace, and to sanctify me. Precisely because he loves me, Jesus calls me by name: he calls me when in prayer he opens to me new horizons of the spiritual life, or when he enables me to know my faults and weaknesses better; he calls me when he reprimands me or purifies me by aridity, as well as when he consoles and encourages me by filling me with new fervor; he calls me when he makes me feel the need of greater generosity, and when he asks me for sacrifices or gives me joys, and still more, when he awakens in me a deeper love for him. Hearing his call, my attitude should be that of a loving little sheep who recognizes the voice of its Shepherd and follows him always.

- Father Gabriel of Saint Mary Magdalen, O.C.D.

In these days, try to keep interiorly occupied with a desire for the coming of the Holy Spirit . . . and with his continual presence. Let your care and esteem for this be so great that nothing else will matter to you or receive your attention, whether it may concern some affliction or some other disturbing memories. And if there be faults in the house during these days, pass over them for the love of the Holy Spirit and of what you owe to the peace and quietude of the soul in which he is pleased to dwell . . . When something distasteful or unpleasant comes your way, remember Christ crucified and be silent. Live in faith and hope, even though you are in darkness, because it is in these darknesses that God protects the soul.

- St. John of the Cross

In his will is our peace. The will of the Savior is that we should help him in his work, becoming suffering servants with him. To the degree that we accept and generously live out this vocation, we shall find peace. However, peace exists at different levels and in various ways within us, for we are wounded in our human nature in ways that Jesus never was . . . "Take me, Lord, battered and half-drowned as I am, and use me. I belong to you for your redemptive work through your Church, the sacrament of salvation for the whole world." This is now our prayer.

- Barbara Dent

God has made us to love, wishes us to love, tells us to love; and his command is without limit. Christ loved to the point of dying . . . Learning to love thus God, our Father, intimately present in the depths of our being and all men, all men together and each in particular, each as a friend, as a real and true brother; learning to love thus, I say, is the first and last thing in the Christian life, and we shall be neither true sons of God's nor true brother to Jesus unless we succeed in doing so. I would go so far as to say that this is the sole problem in your lives - to learn how to love . . . Always have deep respect for every person toward whom your affection may draw you; chaste love is always sensitively respectful. Think of Jesus' love for us, how respectful he is of what we are; and how fragile we could be in his hands. Such, I believe, are the principal characteristics of the love which Jesus will little by little put in your hearts.

- Father Rene Voillaume

God has raised up this little Company, like all others, for his love and good pleasure . . . We have been chosen by God as instruments of his boundless and fatherly love which desires to be established in, and to replenish souls . . . Our vocation, then, is not to go to one parish, or even to one diocese, but throughout the whole world, and for what end? To inflame the hearts of men and women, to do what the Son of God did. He came to cast fire on earth and to inflame it with his love. What else have we to desire save that it burns and consumes all? . . .It is true, then, that I am sent, not merely to love God but to make him loved. It is not enough for me to love God if my neighbor does not love him.

- St. Vincent de Paul

If we really loved the good God, we should make it our joy and happiness to come and spend a few moments to adore him, and ask him for the grace of forgiveness, and we should regard those moments as the happiest of our lives.

- St. John Vianney

The dream of creating a "new heaven and a new earth" lives on. It is not determined by my age, my health, or my degrees, but by my heart and the burning desire to act for God, to make God's love and healing presence visible in a hurting world. I can do something, now, in this time and place. If my eyes and heart are open, I can make a difference, not for the whole world, but for one person or two or twenty. To be in love with God, to follow Christ, means that I must act on behalf of those who need my help. I cannot turn away. I cannot retire. I cannot say, "I have done all that I can do." As long as I can see, I must look for those who are in need. As long as I can talk, I must speak for those who have no voice. As long as I can move, I must act on behalf of justice for the poor. God has given me this time. It is still my time, my time until I die.

- Sister Regina Rogers

God has called you into existence. He wanted to, he meant you to exist. He shaped a life for you, an environment, an education, circumstances, natural gifts, an eternal destiny. You were the subject of his loving forethought, no less deliberately than if you had been the only thing he had created. If God created you so deliberately, thought of you as an individual person, he thinks of you as an individual person still. The Almighty Power, whose word sways the whole of creation, makes you the subject of his loving regard . . . God cares about you as if he had nobody else to care for. God is to be thought of as a Person in a very practical sense - that he knows us, loves us, and does for us. And we are persons so that we may love him, serve him, and do things for him. That is what we are here for; that is our characteristic birthright as human beings.

- Monsignor Ronald Knox

All we can do is flee to God and his mercy. Poor, helpless, frail creatures, we can only beg him to make the crooked straight, to bring low the mountains, to make the darkness light. God stands by us, even if we cannot always be said to have stood by him. He loves us, even if we are sometimes strangely forgetful of him in our daily lives, even if our hearts seem to be more attached to many things than to him, the God of our hearts and our portion forever. He is the one who is faithful to us, good to us, close to us, merciful to us. He is our light. He has come and always longs to come to us more abundantly.

- Karl Rahner

Let us always keep before our eyes the fact that here on earth we are on a battlefield and that in Paradise we shall receive the crown of victory; that this is a testing-ground and the prize will be awarded up above; that we are now in a land of exile while our true homeland is Heaven to which we must continually aspire.

- St. Pio of Pietrelcina

Lord, don't give me riches, don't give me a long or a short life, don't give me powers on earth that make one drunk with power, don't give me the madness of idolatry of the false idols of this world. Cleanse me, Lord. Cleanse my intentions and give me the true wisdom of discernment, so that I may be able to distinguish between good and evil . . .

- Archbishop Oscar Romero

OLord, what is the trust that I can have in this life, or what is my greatest solace among all things under heaven? Is it not you, my Lord God, whose mercy is without measure? When have things been well with me without you, and when have things not been well with me if you were present? I would rather be poor with you than rich without you. I would rather be with you as a pilgrim in this world, than without you in heaven. Where you are is heaven, and where you are not is both death and hell. You are to me, all that I desire, and therefore it is fitting for me to cry to you and heartily to pray to you. I have nothing save you to trust in that can help me in my necessity, for you are my hope, you are my trust, you are my comfort, and you are my most faithful helper in every need.

- Thomas à Kempis

A genuine love of prayer is one of hidden, ordinary holiness and regular duties. Extraordinary spiritual fruitfulness is found in ordinary life . . . We take Jesus to the streets, to the work place, to our families and parish by our love. St. Therese tells us, "In my little way, there will be something for all tastes, except those in extraordinary ways." We become saints by hidden and ordinary virtues. Our stronghold in life is our faith, grounded in Jesus, nourished by prayer and challenged in the service of love.

- Carolyn Humphreys

He (God) is life and power, and as soon as he enters in, he awakens my slumbering soul; he stirs and soothes and pierces my heart, for before it was hard as stone, and diseased. So he has begun to pluck out and destroy, to build up and to plant, to water dry places and to illuminate dark ones; to open what was closed and to warm what was cold; to make the crooked straight and the rough places smooth, so that my soul may bless the Lord, and all that is within me may praise his holy name.

- St. Bernard of Clairvaux

As Christians, our task is to make daily progress toward God. Our pilgrimage on earth is a school in which God is the only teacher, and it demands good students, not ones who play truant. In this school we learn something every day. We learn something from the Commandments, something from examples, and something from the Sacraments. These things are remedies for our wounds and material for our studies.

- St. Augustine

The way in which Christianity looks at things is so very different from the estimate of the world. And so our Lord, by a comparison, makes it clear to his disciples that power, even spiritual power like that which they found themselves to have over the devil, is a small thing compared with the profound issues of our destiny, the more potent things of our faith. What is the thing that matters beyond all else, the thing that should give us utmost joy? It is this: that our names are written in heaven; that we belong to heaven, that we are the children of the Father who is in heaven.

- Father Anscar Vonier, O.S.B.

In 1985, at the invitation of Mayor Koch, Mother Teresa opened a home in New York City for men who were dying of AIDS. Four Missionaries of Charity Sisters dedicated themselves to caring for the fifteen dying men. Mother Teresa named the home, "Gift of Love." The first to pass away there was a man named Harvey. He was a veteran of the Vietnam war and also had a history of drug abuse. One day, Harvey told the Sisters that he would like to be baptized. A priest was summoned and with great joy, the Sisters witnessed the baptism. He also received the Last Rites. "It will be beautiful when you are in heaven," one of the Sisters said. "Yes it will" Harvey replied. "I want to go to heaven but I don't want to leave this home. I have experienced so much love and care here that I never want to leave this place. One day, when one of the Sisters was reading the Psalms to him, Harvey passed away. Like many others who were fortunate enough to receive the help of Mother Teresa and her Missionaries of Charity, Harvey had truly received a gift of love.

Wait upon the Lord; be faithful to his commandments; He will elevate your hope, and put you in possession of his kingdom. Wait upon him patiently; wait upon him by avoiding all sin. He will come, doubt it not; and in the approaching day of his visitation, which will be that of your death and his judgment, he will himself crown your holy hope. Place all your hope in the heart of Jesus; it is a safe asylum; for he who trusts in God is sheltered and protected by his mercy. To this firm hope, join the practice of virtue, and even in this life you will begin to taste the ineffable joys of Paradise.

- St. Bernard of Clairvaux

Patience is long-suffering in injuries, which it endures without trying to return them and without any display of temper. Just as God holds back his anger and delays his punishments in order to give sinners time to repent, so also his sons must overcome their resentment and silence their desire for revenge. Only great love and great humility can give such a victory, especially since Christian patience must be practiced toward everyone and in every possible way. It presupposes great strength of soul . . . Because his patience makes him merciful to those who offend him and courageous in adversity, he lives in interior peace . . . Patience is never bitter . . . If charity is patient in all the irritating happenings of everyday life, it must be by participation through the Holy Spirit, in God's patience and in imitation of Christ's patience.

- Father Ceslaus Spico, O.P.

D o not be frightened . . . by the many things you will need to consider in order to begin this divine journey, which is the royal road to heaven. A great treasure is gained by traveling this road; no wonder we have to pay what seems to us a high price. The time will come when you will understand how trifling everything is next to so precious a reward.

- St. Teresa of Avila

It is important to have a daily time of prayer to Jesus. That is your part. It is up to Jesus then to give the grace to make your time fruitful. And no doubt he sometimes does so by making us feel empty. We do not know the workings of God. We have put forth the effort and that is what Jesus loves. Success or failure is up to him, and we really don't know in prayer what success or failure is. I do not use my time trying to figure out where I am on the spiritual journey. I don't worry about myself at all. I just praise Jesus and thank him. The older I get, the more mysterious life is. I cannot begin to figure it out, or what God is doing with me. I don't understand myself. I never will. It is vain to try to explain the unexplainable and the attempt is consuming time that could be used in giving glory to God. I look on myself simply as a little vigil light trying to burn faithfully. My little flicker of light is praising God. That is what life is for.

- Father Rawley Myers

I have tried to live the gospel and to follow the monastic life each day. I have tried to spend time with God in thought and prayer and reading. God and I have been friends, I might even say, lovers. We live together. My life is in him and he is in my life. It is all kind of simple. I feel a quiet joy and thankfulness. My days and nights are good because God is with me. I get pulled out of my center at times and that usually leads to grief. But then I turn my thoughts back to God and regain my peace. Thank you Lord, for so much more than I deserve. Amen

- Father Basil Pennington, O.C.S.O.

Silence is a necessity for a contemplative soul, and there can be no prayer without it. To each of us is given the obligation to make our cloister and our soul a house of prayer, the home of the Blessed Trinity, a sanctuary of God, where we may pass our life listening to him and learning all from him. Let us be watchful over interior silence, especially. We are all aware how easily a slight contradiction may call up a multitude of persons and things to occupy our minds. These are "intruders" we are letting into the sanctuary, causing us to lose sight of the Divine Guest therein and to lose precious time with things that in no way concern his glory. We must bring back our souls to silence and solitude as soon as such thoughts arise to disturb the peace of our interior sanctuary.

- Mother Aloysius of the Blessed Sacrament

L et us remain in the care of the Shepherd, and we shall remain there, if we listen to his voice, if we obey him, if we do not follow anyone else. Now, what is his voice like? *Blessed are the poor in spirit; blessed are the pure of heart; blessed are the merciful.* If we put these beatitudes into practice, we shall remain in the care of the Shepherd, and the wolf will be unable to come inside the fold. However, even if he should attack, he will do this for his own destruction, for we have a Shepherd who loves us so dearly as to lay down his life for us. Therefore, since he is powerful and since he loves us, what prevents us from being saved? Nothing - unless we ourselves should put an obstacle in the way . . . Listen to him saying, *You cannot serve two masters, God and mammon.* Therefore, if we serve the one, we shall not be subject to the tyranny of the other.

- St. John Chrysostom

This, then, is the time, dear friend, when it is necessary for us to be completely consumed in the Sacred Heart of our Divine Master. We must never leave him . . . After we have lost our sinful heart in the divine flames of this pure love, we must assume a completely new one . . . This new heart must have quite new sentiments and new affections. There must be nothing of self left in it. This Divine Heart of Jesus must so completely take the place of ours that only he will live and act in us and for us. His will must annihilate ours so that he can act without resistance on our part. His actions, his thoughts, his desires must take the place of ours, but most of all his love . . . And so we shall be able to say with St. Paul, that we live no more, but Christ lives in us.

- St. Margaret Mary Alacoque

Remember that your soul is a temple of the living God. *The kingdom of God is within you.* Night and day let your aim be to remain in simplicity and gentleness, calmness and serenity, and in freedom from created things, so that you will find your joy in the Lord Jesus. Love silence and solitude, even when in the midst of a crowd or when caught up in your work. Physical solitude is a good thing, provided that it is backed up by prayer and a holy life, but far better than this is solitude of the heart, which is the interior desert in which your spirit can become totally immersed in God, and can hear and savor the words of eternal life. With great purity of intention, aim in everything to do what pleases God. Always remain faithful to God and genuinely accept whatever he wishes.

- St. Paul of the Cross

You recall the immensely profound saying of St. John of the Cross, "In the evening of life, we will be judged on love." This love expresses itself in constant prayer. I say "constant" because this state of prayer must be our life not for only two hours a day, but all day long. Our life must be a constant, silent prayer that rises unceasingly to God. That is what constitutes our duty in life - prayer is our primary duty. Prayer is the reason why God has placed us on earth. We learn truly to pray, when we are in the presence and company of Christ. Therefore, we must contemplate Christ for long periods of time and seek him persistently.

- Pere Jacques

The whole plan of our spiritual life is a loving union and intimate partnership with Jesus in which we return him love for love . . . In giving himself to us, he gives us his Holy Spirit to dwell in our souls, as a permanent friend and source of strength and light . . . He has made the whole spiritual life a partnership with himself, making us part of himself, and he has reduced our share in the work of the partnership to a minimum. In fact, to repeat Father Clerissac's words: "It is our emptiness and trust that he needs, not our plentitude." All he asks is that we put our faith and hope in him, that we love him with our whole heart, that we renounce our own pretended strength and our foolish plans by humility and abandonment; he will do the rest.

- Father Eugene Boylan, O.C.S.O.

O Lord, we ask for boundless confidence and trust in your divine mercy, and the courage to accept the crosses and sufferings which bring immense goodness to our souls and that of your church. Help us to love you with a pure and contrite heart, and to humble ourselves beneath your cross, as we climb the mountain of holiness, carrying our cross that leads to heavenly glory. May we receive you with great faith and love in Holy Communion, and allow you to act in us as you desire for your greater glory. O Jesus, most adorable Heart and eternal fountain of Divine Love, may our prayer find favor before the Divine Majesty of your Heavenly Father. Amen

- St. Pio of Pietrelcina

The Lord is such a good Father that he anticipates our desire to be pardoned and comes forward to us, opening his arms laden with grace . . . When God runs toward us, we cannot keep silent, but with St. Paul we exclaim: *Abba, Pater*: "Father, my Father.". . .He wants us to call him Father; he wants us to savor that word, our souls filled with joy. Human life is in some way a constant returning to our Father's house. We return through contrition, through the conversion of heart, which means a desire to change, a firm decision to improve our life and which, therefore, is expressed in sacrifice and self giving. God is waiting for us, like the father in the parable, with open arms, even though we don't deserve it. It doesn't matter how great our debt is. Just like the prodigal son, all we have to do is open our heart, to be homesick for our Father's house, to wonder at and rejoice in the gift which God gives us, of being able to call ourselves his children, of really being his children, even though our response to him has been so poor.

- St. Josemaría Escrivá

I can only face the fact of the horror of human suffering because of the presence of the Holy One in the middle of all our pain. The agony of my own country is, for me, only bearable because Christ, the Innocent One, was crucified and hung up to die, while his love remained unbroken and undefeated. This enables me to go on loving, hoping, and planting new crops. In Christ's name and in his power I pray that we shall all find strength to let love, and not hate, win the day.

- A minister of Mozambique, Africa

There was a scaffold in a courtyard of our prison in Dachau's concentration camp. I used to look at it every day and receive its sermon and had to pray a good many times because of this sermon. It was not that I was afraid of being hanged on the scaffold one fine morning - one becomes accustomed even to this prospect, as we all get used to the idea of having to die one day. No, what scared me was what I might do at the crucial moment. Would I cry out with my last breath, "You are making me die like a criminal but you Nazis are the real criminals. There's a God in heaven and some day he'll prove it to you!" If I were to die like that, even in the name of Christ, I would die an unbeliever, not believing that the prayer Jesus prayed on the Cross was meant for me, too. For none of us can live by the grace of God, or be fully reconciled to him, unless, at the same time, we offer mercy and forgiveness to our fellow human beings.

- Martin Niemoller

If you consider the poor in the light of faith, you will observe that they are taking the place of the Son of God who chose to be poor . . . Christ made himself the servant of the poor and shared their poverty. He went so far as to say that he would consider every deed which either helps or harms the poor as done for or against himself. Since God surely loves the poor, he also loves those who love the poor. That is why we hope that God will love us for the sake of the poor . . . Therefore, we must try to be stirred by our neighbors' worries and distress. We must beg God to pour into our hearts sentiments of pity and compassion and to fill them again and again with these dispositions . . . Charity is certainly greater than any rule. Moreover, all rules must lead to charity. With renewed devotion, then, we must serve the poor, especially outcasts and beggars.

- St. Vincent de Paul

Our chief and constant prayer must be the willed offering of our depths to God's secret action. He is working to dredge up what needs purifying, his performance rather like that of a soundless excavator, throwing up rubble as it goes along . . . He says, "Let me act. Be still. Don't struggle. Don't have any of your own ideas about how this excavation should proceed. Just leave it to me and trust in the midst of absurdity." In the passive purgations, God is working to produce a state of total dependence in us. He wants us to be spiritual infants in his arms. We hurt because our self-will still strives to be in control of our lives, and we struggle to evade God's embrace, which only makes him hold us tighter. He is teaching us, not by words or clearly understood concepts, but by stamping the seal of his grace upon our deepest selves.

- Barbara Dent

S t. Augustine . . . describes very beautifully the intimate relationship between prayer and hope. He defines prayer as an exercise of desire. Man was created for greatness – for God himself; he was created to be filled by God. But his heart is too small for the greatness to which it is destined. It must be stretched . . . He then uses a very beautiful image to describe this process of enlargement and preparation of the human heart. "Suppose that God wishes to fill you with honey (a symbol of God's tenderness and goodness); but if you are full of vinegar, where will you put the honey? The vessel, that is your heart, must first be enlarged and then cleansed" . . . This requires hard work and is painful, but in this way alone do we become suited to that for which we are destined.

- Pope Benedict XVI

Our vocation is to belong to Jesus. The easiest way and the simplest way of belonging is this: The Holy Spirit makes us do that giving of self, that total surrender to God, without any reflection, without any counting the cost. We call that "blind surrender.". . .The whole of our life must come to that one word, "yes." Yes to God - that is holiness. We allow God to take from us whatever he wants and we accept whatever he gives with a big smile. That is "yes" in action. Yes means I surrender totally, fully, without counting the cost, without any examination, "Is it all right? Is it convenient?" Our yes to God is without any reservations. I belong to him so totally there are no reservations. It doesn't matter what we feel.

- *Mother Teresa of Calcutta*

I will try to find a new way to heaven, quite short and direct. We live in an age of inventions. We need no longer climb laboriously up flights of stairs; in well-to-do houses there are lifts. And I was determined to find a lift to carry me to Jesus, for I was far too small to climb the steep stairs of perfection. So I sought in Holy Scripture some idea of what this life I wanted would be, and I read these words, *Whosoever is a little one, let him come to me.* It is your arms, O Jesus, that are the lift to carry me to heaven. And so there is no need for me to grow up. I must stay little and become less and less.

- *St. Therese of Lisieux*

Nothing is so beautiful as a pure soul . . . Purity comes from heaven; we must ask for it from God. If we ask for it, we shall obtain it. We must take great care not to lose it. We must shut our heart against pride, against sensuality, and all the other passions, as one shuts the doors and windows that nobody may be able to get in. What joy it is to the guardian angel to conduct a pure soul! . . . The more pure we have been on earth, the nearer we shall be to him in heaven . . . My children, we cannot comprehend the power that a pure soul has over the good God.

- St. John Vianney

I am the vine and you are the branches . . . and everyone that bears fruit, he will purge it that it may bring forth much fruit (John 15:1-2). This purging or pruning action of the Father is what disconcerts us. We see an orchard in full bloom, and what has a more delicate charm? And yet those flowers must disappear if the branches are to bring forth fruit. There are many flowers in our life that seem of great value to us. In God's sight they are only flowers, and in his mercy, he removes them that we may yield him fruit . . . The whole trouble is that, literally, we do not know what is good for us; and what makes the trouble still worse is that we think we do. We have our own plans for our happiness and too often we merely regard God as somebody who will help us to accomplish them. The true state of affairs is just the opposite. God has his plans for our happiness, and he is waiting for us to help him to accomplish them. And let us be quite clear about it, we cannot improve on God's plans. Once a man has realized that God wills his happiness and that all that happens to him is ruled and regulated by God with infinite wisdom and power toward that end, and that all God asks of him is to cooperate with that loving will of his, then that man has found the beginning of peace.

- Father Eugene Boylan, O.C.S.O.

God approaches gently, often secretly, always in love . . . He comes to us, as he himself has told us, in those whom we know in our own lives. Very often we do not recognize him. He comes in many people we do not like, in all who need what we can give, in all who have something to give us, and for our greater comfort. He comes in those we love, in our fathers and mothers, our brothers and sisters, our friends and our children. Because this is so, we must not be content ever to love with only natural love. We must also love everyone with a supernatural, sacramental love.

- Caryll Houselander

Joy in human life has to do with God . . . Only in God is man fully capable of life. Without him, over time, we become sick. This sickness attacks our joy and our capability for joy . . . In order to be capable of true life, man must live according to a specific order and relationship to God . . . Man should take joy as seriously as he takes himself. And he should believe in himself, believe in his heart and in his Lord God, even through darkness and distress - that he is created for joy . . . We are created for a life that knows itself to be blessed, sent, and touched at its deepest center by God Himself.

- Father Alfred Delp, S.J.

Whatever the work with which you have been entrusted - as a religious, as a layperson - it is a means for you to put your love for God in a living action, in an action of love . . . Every time you smile at someone, it is an action of love, a gift to that person, a beautiful thing . . . So if I want to know how much I love Christ, if I want to know if I am really in love with God, then I have only to look at how I do the work he has entrusted to me - how much love I put into the doing of that work. You see, it is not the work in itself that is our vocation - our vocation is to belong totally to Jesus . . . What you are doing, I may not be able to do . . . What I am doing, you may not be able to do . . . but all of us together are doing something beautiful for God.

- Mother Teresa of Calcutta

Oh Jesus, let us always fear and love your holy name because you never take away your guidance from those whom are founded in the firmness of your love. A greater grace than the love of God has never been granted to any human being. It comprises our true life; it is our happiness, the peace of our restless hearts, the content of our eternity. Shouldn't we pray for this love? Won't the Father hear us when we request nothing else from him than that he take us to his heart, when we desire no other wealth than his love?

- Karl Rahner

To do things for God, to serve him - that will follow naturally from our love. It is possible to serve God by reminding ourselves that he is our creator and we ought to do his will unquestioningly. Or we can serve him by reminding ourselves that he is our King and that any homage which we offer to him is only his right. But the best way of all is to serve him because he is our Friend, because we want to profess our love for him by our actions. That is what God made us for, his human creatures, to be his friends, his personal friends.

- Monsignor Ronald Knox

For everything is in God – the remedies for your wounds, the help which you need, the correction of your faults, the source of your progress. In a word, all that one can and should wish for. There is no reason to ask the Word for anything other than himself, since he is all things.

- St. Bernard of Clairvaux

How are we to be reborn and become whole? By finding our true center which is God, finding God in all things, and the desire for God in all desires, and so beginning to live the life of worship instead of the life of self-worship. But this in its turn implies a precedent turning away from the false self, an acknowledgment of our essential insufficiency; and because of our state of sin, an acknowledgment of our need of a Savior without whom we cannot, in our bondage, turn away from ourselves . . . We find God by realizing, in the first place, our need of God, as a child realizes its need of a father.

- Father Gerald Vann, O.P.

O ne of the most important things you can do to improve your spiritual life and your mental health is to fill your mind with uplifting thoughts. If you hold on to hurtful memories, they will only make you sick. You have a choice. You can reject them. Decide firmly that you will not let the past drag you down. Turn to the Lord and ask for help. Pray for the grace to come into the present moment. You don't have to work endlessly through the toxic effects of the past. Once you decide to change, the process can begin. St. Teresa of Avila used to repeat to herself over and over, "Let nothing disturb you. Let nothing cause you fear. God is unchanging. God will suffice." With the Lord at your side, you can do all things. Remember the words of Jesus, *I have told you all these things that your joy may be full* (John 15:11).

- Father John Catoir

Today we suffer from a deadly cancer: the incapacity to love . . . Yes, love generates love, and today there is an immense need of persons able to generate hope in love. We experience resurrection every day with the lost and dead youth who enter our houses, as well as with their families who have been destroyed by suffering and desperation . . . Daily we live an experience of hope that gives life to those from whom life has been stolen. Because of this, we believe that in the darkest night, it is possible to find light again. Even in the darkest sadness, joy can be rekindled. Even in the bitterest loneliness, a friend's love can pierce a hardened heart. Yes, we want to be witnesses of this hope. We want to announce to this world that the secret of rebirth is to open our hearts to that marvelous Father who waits for each of us as his most precious child.

- Mother Elvira Petrozzi

*F*east of St. *Edward the Confessor* Edward grew up in innocence, delighting chiefly in assisting at Mass and in association with the clergy. In 1041, when Edward was forty years old, he was raised to the throne of England. The virtues of his earlier years - simplicity, gentleness, humility and charity, but above all his angelic purity, shone with new brightness. He loved to stand at his palace gate, speaking kindly to the poor beggars and lepers who crowded about him, many of whom were healed by his touch. Being devoid of personal ambition, Edward's one aim was the welfare of his people. His reign of twenty-four years was one of almost unbroken peace. One man who knew St. Edward said of him, "He was devoted to God and directed by God. He lived the life of an angel in the administration of his kingdom." Edward died on January 5, 1066. Many miracles occurred at his tomb. In 1102 his body was exhumed and found to be incorrupt. He was canonized in 1161. St. Edward the Confessor is the patron saint of difficult marriages, separated spouses, and kings.

It is a great advantage to have a room or a corner of a room . . . reserved for the discipline of solitude . . . There we dwell in the presence of the Lord. Our temptation is to do something useful - to read something stimulating, to think about something interesting, or to experience something unusual. But our moment of solitude is precisely a moment in which we want to be in the presence of our Lord with empty hands, naked, vulnerable, useless, without much to show, prove, or defend . . . Although the discipline of solitude asks us to set aside time and space, what finally matters is that our hearts become like quiet cells where God can dwell, wherever we go and whatever we do. The more we train ourselves to spend time with God and him alone, the more we will discover that God is with us at all times and in all places. Then we will be able to recognize him even in the midst of a busy and active life. Once the solitude of time and space has become a solitude of the heart, we will never have to leave that solitude. We will be able to live the spiritual life in any place and any time. Thus the discipline of solitude enables us to live active lives in the world, while remaining always in the presence of the living God.

- Henri Nouwen

Let your desire be to see God; your fear, that you may lose him; your sorrow, that you are not having fruition of him; your joy, that he can bring you to himself. Thus you will live in great peace.

- St. Teresa of Avila

W̶e are called to love God above all things with our whole heart and soul and mind . . . Love is choosing. I have to choose to love God when my conscious being feels no attraction save for what is here and now desirable . . . I am loving much when I pour out my love over the feet of Jesus in his brethren. I have to bring before my mind all sorts of reasons for doing this . . . But there are other powerful incentives that perhaps have to precede the loving preoccupation with Jesus: consideration of the brevity of our life-span, its mysteriousness, what it is for, its gravity, and the appalling danger of wasting it. All day long, if we take the trouble, we can glean in the field of our lives, abundant motives for surrendering ourselves to life's whole meaning - God.

- Sister Ruth Burrows

Slowly we begin to discover the treasures in silence. We hear the word of God in the milieu of silence. Out of that milieu, God spoke one word through which the world was created and redeemed. We are quietly receptive to this word and through it we gradually learn to be attentive to truth. What whets the appetite for spiritual nourishment? It is silence. When we become aware of this, a time for silence in our daily lives becomes essential . . . Meister Eckhart (14th century Christian mystic) wrote: "There is nothing more like God than silence." We become content with the silence of God outside or inside of prayer. Through and in silence, we stand still before God and we find the beauty of his reality. The silence of God's love is too great for any expression. The book of Wisdom tells us, *When night was at its deepest point and all was stilled and silent, your word oh Lord, came down.* To this word we listen, respond to love, and live and listen again.

- Carolyn Humphreys

We must not only have faith in the Lord, but must wait on him; not only must hope, but must watch for him; not only love him, but must long for him; not only obey him, but must look out, look up earnestly for our reward, which is himself. We must not only make him the object of our faith, hope, and charity, but we must make it our duty not to believe the world, not to hope in the world, not to love the world. We must resolve not to hang on the world's opinion, or study its wishes. It is our mere wisdom to be thus detached from all things below.

- Blessed John Henry Newman

October 19

Bless us in all we think and do, seeking to know the light of your truth, Lord, and to taste of your love. The world is too much with us; help us to get nearer to you and to the things and thoughts that die not, evermore. You have promised that you will hear and answer the prayers of your children in their needs. Save us from ourselves at all times, O God, and keep us for your kingdom.

- Lauchlan Maclean Watt

October 20

God stands at the center of our lives just as Jesus stands at the center of the Gospel story. Jesus is the source of the gift of healing, but he is easily forgotten. He does not force himself into the lives of the ten lepers. Only one of them makes the connection between his good fortune and the role Jesus plays in it, and he is the one you would least expect to make it. The story of the ten lepers . . . teaches us that not only do most people forget who they are, but that the one who remembers is . . . someone whom we think can teach us nothing. And yet in the story, he is the only one who shines. He is the only one with real insight into life. God is central to our personal story, but he is easily forgotten. God will not usually overwhelm us. Jesus portrays God as knocking at the door of our lives, waiting to enter. He will not come uninvited.

- Father Brendan Freeman, O.C.S.O.

The Holy Spirit has been sent into our hearts, awakening us to the Father's call for us to be one with him in Christ. The very love that unites the Father and the Son stirs within us, and with unutterable groanings inflames the will to seek no other gratification than perfect communion with God . . . Because I am blind, I do not see this touch of love that has claimed my heart. Because my faith is weak, I doubt the power that has been awakened within me. Because I am confused by all my compromises and attachments, I continue to delay in embracing the wisdom of surrendering completely to this touch. But God never gives up on me. He continues to renew in unexpected ways, my awareness of his presence within and around me, calling me to union.

- James Finley

All that the friends of Christ did for him in his lifetime, we can do . . . We do it by seeing Christ and serving Christ in friends and strangers, in everyone we come in contact with . . . He said that a glass of water given to a beggar was given to him. He made heaven hinge on the way we act toward him in his disguise of commonplace, frail, ordinary humanity . . . And to those who say, aghast, that they never had a chance to do such a thing, that they lived two thousand years too late, he will say again what they had a chance of knowing all their lives, that if these things were done for the very least of his brethren, they were done to him.

- Dorothy Day

Happiness consists in knowing what you want, and then knowing you have it, or you are on the way to getting it. What we want is God. Our hearts will not rest until they rest in you, O Lord. Our minds seek infinite truth. Our hearts are made for infinite love. The purpose of the structures of our life - of going apart from the world in silence, in solitude - is so that we can keep alive, at that level of knowing, who we are and what we really want. Through contemplative prayer and spiritual experiences, we then know that, to some extent, we have it now or are on the way of getting it. This is the meaning of Cistercian life; we are on the way. We have committed ourselves . . . That is why our life can be tremendously happy. There is a deep joy. We know what we want, and we know, to some extent, that we already enjoy it but there is infinitely more in eternal life. We are on the way to it.

- Father Basil Pennington, O.C.S.O.

There is death which is separation of body and soul - physical death. But there is also a death which is separation between man and God. This is spiritual death. Spiritual death befalls a person who deliberately chooses to live as if God did not exist . . . This spiritual life, sometimes called supernatural life, more often called grace - God wants to give to us all. He wants to give us that life, whereby here and now, we can enjoy friendship with him and ultimately be guaranteed the vision of God which alone . . . can satisfy our deepest aspirations. He wants to give us life; and he wants to renew that gesture whereby he restored life to the son of the widow of Naim, to the daughter of Jairus, to his friend Lazarus. To them, he restored physical life; to us, by a like gesture, he restores spiritual life . . . If we choose to reject it, then dearest brethren, we live "dead," we live a life which is fundamentally meaningless because it is bound by horizons of this present world, destined ultimately to frustration, to misery. To live separated from God is indeed to live "dead."

- Cardinal Basil Hume

G od has given me the gift of being responsible for the Portiuncula, the chapel on campus that is set aside for adoration. I believe as caretaker of this chapel, God is calling me to Perpetual Adoration. This means that I am to adore Jesus in the Eucharist whether I am in the Portiuncula or not. I have been doing this by adoring him in spirit from wherever I am . . . I personally believe that Eucharistic Adoration should become our highest priority. If we can remove the veil that hides Jesus in the Eucharist, we will more easily find him in all the other ways he desires to be present with us.

- Father Sam Tiesi

I t is good to empty your memory of all visible things, and to fill it again with the hope of heavenly things. Even here, how happy we are. There are many miseries, no doubt, our sins especially and the long procession of our imperfections and our weaknesses. But when one thinks that our beloved Jesus is always with us in the Tabernacle . . . that he is always in our souls, what can we say . . . but that life has lost its darkness . . . Dear brothers in Jesus, how lucky we are.

- Blessed Charles de Foucauld

We must be sure that our heart bears no malice and is full of good will to people. All of this demands humility and an intense personal love of our Lord. That is the secret for all of your problems. Instead of tackling our failures directly, the best way is to tackle them indirectly by going to our Lord - reading about him, thinking about him, and talking to him and to his mother. Ask our Lady to give you the grace of close familiar friendship with our Lord. It is good to reflect on why God has called you to monastic life. God brought you to the monastery to love him. You show that love by loving your brethren with a supernatural love based on love for his Son, our Lord Jesus Christ.

- Father Eugene Boylan, O.C.S.O.

Oh how easily we could win heaven - day by day - just by doing what we have to do, but doing it for God.

- St. John Vianney

Love of God is a divinely infused virtue which leads us to love the Lord our God as the sovereign good, and purely for his own sake . . . The happiness of the elect in heaven consists in seeing and loving God. Our happiness here on earth must likewise consist in loving and seeing our Lord, not indeed face to face as the saints and angels do, but by means of the light of faith. Thus we begin in this valley of tears, this earthly exile, the life of the blessed in heaven, a life of endless joy in the fruition of the vision of God.

- St. Alphonsus Liguori

We must learn to trust God, because this is what Christ taught. He told us to live in the present. His whole teaching stresses that idea . . . He tells us not to save up, or make any provision for the future, to live in the moment. But we seldom do so . . . No, we grieve because of what tomorrow may bring . . . But trust does not mean believing that God will spare us from suffering . . . To trust God means that we must know that whatever comes to us comes from his hand . . . Christ says, *Take no thought of tomorrow.* He also says, *Take up your cross daily.* There is no need, in accepting sorrow, to look ahead, to imagine tomorrow, to ask for more or less, but just as we receive our joy day by day, so can we receive our sorrow day by day, and it will be measured day by day, by the love of God and our own littleness . . . To look for God's gift in the moment is the way to learn to trust.

- Caryll Houselander

He who learns to live the interior life and to take little account of outward things, does not seek special places or times to perform devout exercises. A spiritual man quickly recollects himself because he has never wasted his attention upon externals. No outside work, no business that cannot wait stands in his way. He adjusts himself to things as they happen. He, whose disposition is well ordered, cares nothing about the strange, perverse behavior of others, for a man is upset and distracted only in proportion as he engrosses himself in externals.

- Thomas à Kempis

I was going further and further from you, my Lord and my life, and so my life was turning into death. And in this state of death you still watched over me. You made me feel a painful emptiness, a sadness the like of which I've never felt before or since . . . How good you are. How you kept me safe. How you sheltered me under your wings when I didn't even believe you existed!

- Blessed Charles de Foucauld

Look at the trees of the forest. See how sturdy and beautiful they are, how tall they grow, and how smooth is their bark. Yet when we plant a garden, we prefer other kinds of trees, such as pomegranate and olive trees. This is because we want trees that bear fruit. We are the trees which God has planted in his garden. He is not concerned at how sturdy and beautiful we are, at how tall we grow, or at how smooth our skin is. As trees in his garden, he is concerned only that we bear fruit. And the fruit which he wants us to bear is spiritual: peace and love, faith and gentleness, patience and self-control, generosity and loyalty . . . He has planted us on this earth not for our own sakes, but for his glory; and we can only glorify him by the spiritual fruits that grow in our souls.

- St. John Chrysostom

Difficulties are the voice of God speaking to us. God speaks to us through events, through circumstances. And when these are hard to bear, he is trying to make us less reliant upon ourselves, teaching us to have more confidence in him . . . We make a great error in the religious life if we do not learn, if we do not accept in our hearts, that difficulties are not obstacles between God and ourselves - they are the way to him. We make a great mistake if we fail to realize that this carrying of the Cross is totally compatible with peace, serenity, and happiness.

- Cardinal Basil Hume

There should be, even in the busiest day, a few moments when we can close our eyes and let God possess us. He is always present, always giving us life, always round us and in us, like the air we breathe; there should be moments at least when we become more conscious of his presence; when we become conscious of it as the only reality, the only thing that will last forever.

- Caryll Houselander

The Word of God is sacramental. That means it is sacred, and as a sacred word, it makes present what it indicates . . . When we say that God's Word is sacred, we mean that God's Word is full of God's presence. The questions therefore are: How does God come to me as I listen to the Word? Where do I discern the healing hand of God touching me through the Word? How are my sadness, my grief and my mourning being transformed at this very moment? Do I sense the fire of God's love purifying my heart and giving me new life? These questions lead me to the sacrament of the Word, the sacred place of God's real presence . . . When Jesus joins us on the road and explains the scriptures to us, we must listen with our whole being, trusting that the Word that created us will also heal us. God wants to become present to us and thus radically transform our fearful hearts.

- Henri Nouwen

It is for the sake of this purity of heart that we must do all that we do and seek all that we seek. For the sake of purity of heart we seek solitude, fasting, vigils, labors, poor clothing, reading, and all the other monastic virtues. Through these practices we hope to be able to keep our heart untouched by the assaults of all the passions, and by these steps we hope to ascend to perfect love.

- John Cassian

Jesus has done ninety-nine percent of what is necessary to make us saints. He is quite prepared to do the other one percent, but we will not let him. What did he cry for over Jerusalem? *How often I would have gathered your children together, as a hen gathers her young under her wings, but you would not let me* (Luke 13:34). That is our trouble. We will not be gathered under his wings. We want to be big fellows. We want to have something big on our tombstone: This man did so and so. We will not trust our Lord. We will not accept the truth about our weaknesses and admit that we need our Lord. In every other walk of life, progress is associated with independence. The more competent you are, the more independent you are. The one exception is the spiritual life. The more you progress in the spiritual life, the more completely dependent you become on God.

- Father Eugene Boylan, O.C.S.O.

We must relearn our devotion to the Cross. It seems too passive to us, too pessimistic, too sentimental - but if we have not been devoted to the Cross of Jesus in our lifetime, how will we endure our own cross when the time comes for it to be laid upon us? A friend of mine, who depended for years on kidney dialysis and who realized that his life was slipping away from him moment by moment, once told me that as a child, and later as an adult, he had a special devotion to the Way of the Cross and had often prayed it. When he heard the frightening diagnosis of his illness, he was at first stunned; then suddenly the thought came to him: what you have prayed so often has now become a reality in your life; now you can really accompany Jesus; you have been joined to him by his Way of the Cross. In this way, my friend recovered his serenity, which thereafter illuminated his countenance to the end of his days.

- Pope Benedict XVI

Without our suffering, our work would just be social work, very good and helpful, but it would not be the work of Jesus Christ, not part of the redemption. Jesus wanted to help us by sharing our life, our loneliness, our agony and death . . . We are allowed to do the same - all the desolation of the poor people, not only their material poverty, but their spiritual destitution, must be redeemed and we must have our share in it. Pray thus when you find it hard - "I wish to live in this world which is so far from God, which is turned so much from the light of Jesus, to help the poor, to take upon myself some of their suffering."

- Mother Teresa of Calcutta

If . . . you know your own need for mercy, they your eyes will be turned on God. You will be able to be the instrument of his own gift of pity, and so you will give new heart to others. You will not only console but strengthen and sustain. Happy are the merciful, for they shall obtain mercy. To obtain mercy, says St. Thomas, is more even than to have one's fill, because it means that man receives more than he merited or was able to desire. If we have the sense of sin, we want God's mercy; and to receive that is much indeed; but we need his mercy more than we want it, for we need it more than we can know.

- Father Gerald Vann, O.P.

Our present life is given to us only to gain the eternal one and if we don't think about it, we build our affections on what belongs to this world, where our life is transitory. When we have to leave it, we are afraid and become agitated. Believe me, to live happily in this pilgrimage, we have to aim at the hope of arriving at our Homeland, where we will stay eternally. Meanwhile, we have to believe firmly that God calls us to himself and follows us along the path toward him. He will never permit anything to happen to us that is not for our greater good. He knows who we are and he will hold out his paternal hand to us during difficulties, so that nothing will prevent us from running to him swiftly. But to enjoy this grace we must have complete trust in him.

- St. Pio of Pietrelcina

We look around us at a world of noise and frenzied activity, of blaring voices in the media clamoring for attention, and millions of daily words poured out in print demanding to be read. We see the streets of our cities crowded with people and moving vehicles. We look at the sky and see planes traveling at speeds that were not even dreamed of at the beginning of the last century. We find ourselves surrounded by human beings who are preoccupied with money and pleasure and having a good time, and then we wonder: How can a believer in Christ be his devoted follower in an age that seems to be oblivious to heaven and eternity and everything Jesus stands for? Here are two recommendations: Learn the secret of silence, and develop the art of mental prayer. Together, this will give us some idea of how Christ can, and must be followed in our day.

- Father John Hardon

Being holy means living exactly as our Father in heaven wants us to live. You will say that it is difficult. It is. The ideal is a very high one. And yet it is also easy. It is within our reach. When a person becomes ill, there may be no appropriate medicine. But in supernatural affairs, it is not like that. The medicine is always at hand. It is Jesus Christ, present in the Holy Eucharist, and he also gives us his grace in the other sacraments which he established. Let us say again, in word and in action: "Lord, I trust in you; your ordinary providence, your help each day, is all I need."

- St. Josemaría Escrivá

What our Lord does is always best. Now I am happy with my calling. I have made a complete sacrifice of myself to our dear Savior. I feel that even if I cannot be active, still our Savior will take my life as my activity . . . I have only one wish and that is to be the cause of nothing but joy to our Savior and never to hurt him.

- *Therese Neumann*

In Bourke, Australia, Mother Teresa and her Sisters visited and assisted the poor and infirm. In one small hut was an elderly man who lived alone. Mother Teresa cleaned his hut and washed his clothes. One day she found a very dusty lamp among his possessions. She asked the man if he ever lit it and he told her that he did not. "I have not had a visitor for years and years," the man said. "There is no reason for me to light the lamp." Will you light the lamp if my Sisters come and visit you?" Mother Teresa asked. The man replied that he would. Mother Teresa cleaned the lamp and arranged for her Sisters to visit him every evening. He grew to look forward to their visits and always had the lamp lit for them. Two years passed and Mother Teresa forgot about the incident. One day, she received a message from the man. He said, "Tell my friend, Mother Teresa, that the light she lit in my life is still burning."

This life is precious in that it reveals to us the existence and attributes of Almighty God. It is precious because it enables us to know other immortal souls who are on trial like we are. It is momentous as being the scene and means of our trial - but beyond that, life has no claim upon us. We may be rich or poor, young or old, honored or slighted, and it ought to affect us no more than an actor in a play. The one desire which should move us all is the desire to see God face to face.

- Blessed John Henry Newman

This is how we want to pray, "Let me love you, my God. What do I have in heaven, what on earth other than you, God of my heart and my share in eternity? Let me cling to you. Beloved Lord, be the center of my heart. Purify it so that it loves you. Let my happiness be your blessedness, your beauty, your goodness and holiness. Be always with me, and when I am tempted to leave you, my God, do not let me . . . Your love is the highest ideal. Never let it cease; without it I am nothing. Let me be united with you one day eternally through love."

- Karl Rahner

Now, Christian hope creates with us a capacity to desire and to receive what by ourselves we would be unable to desire, receive or even to recognize . . . Hope is like the constant breathing of this life. We breathe in order to live. There is no particular age or hour for breathing. We don't quit breathing so that we can work . . . Christian hope, hopes for Jesus Christ, hopes for God. What God was yesterday, he still is today and will be tomorrow. And Jesus Christ has been raised from the dead forever. Hope, in our interior life, possesses an extraordinary activity and effectiveness. It allows us, by the dust of lowly battles, efforts, and labors, to transform the circumstances or events of our life into eternal events.

- Madeleine Delbrel

Man's great, true hope which holds firm in spite of all disappointments can only be God - God who has loved us and who continues to love us "to the end," until all "is finished." Whoever is moved by love begins to perceive what "life" really is . . . Life in its true sense is not something we have exclusively in or from ourselves; it is a relationship. And life in its totality is a relationship with him who is the source of life. If we are in relation with him who does not die, who is Life itself and Love itself, then we are in life. Then we "live."

- Pope Benedict XVI

Coming to Mass on Sunday is to come to make our alliance with God real. Each Sunday Mass is living the alliance that teaches me to respect God . . . Facing him, I have to dethrone all of the idols that want to take God's place in my heart: the idols of power, of wealth, of licentiousness - the idols of all of these things that separate men from God. Sunday has to be for us, the alliance with the Lord that is renewed.

- Archbishop Oscar Romero

We long for truth; we love it and endlessly search for it, because it is the goal of our being . . . A voice resounds near us, the all-powerful Word of invitation that lifts us up and transforms us: *I am the way, and the truth, and the life* (John 14:6). Let us walk in the awareness of this voice. He who can speak such words will never deceive us . . . The gratuitous search for beauty, the passionate concern for justice, the love of truth, are so many paths that lead to God. Sometimes we make many detours; we even get lost a little . . . There is nothing so great or ideally beautiful as the action of God in the human soul. If we knew how to discern it in ourselves, our lives would be transformed.

- Elisabeth Leseur

In the degrees of humility, there is always a question of the inner person, the heart. We progress to the interior, where I know myself and know that I am known by God . . . This knowledge is always an awareness of my "creatureliness" - that is, I have not brought myself into being, that another has caused me to be and that other is God himself . . . My purpose is to become a person who worships God through and through . . . It supposes the essence of humility - a constant contact with my nature, a constant mindfulness of the fact that I cannot be at the center of my universe, but it must be God who is the center.

- Father Simon O'Donnell, O.S.B

Once we are with the gospel Christ, the gaze of faith, the mutual presence in love, maintains a living contact. It puts us in place before the radiating gaze of the living God. We are asked to be awake there. We can rest there . . . In that contact God is building up his life in us, communicating himself to us. . . Beyond praise, petition, or begging for pardon, the impulse in prayer is towards presence, being with, being with the Person. This must be so. Otherwise, we would be cheated of our Christian inheritance. The Son who elected to "be with" us has opened new possibilities in prayer. In the gospels people do indeed ask Jesus for things, and praise him for his ministry. But there is a deeper movement, expressed by the attitude of the sinners whose concern is to "sit with" him, whose happiness is to know themselves "received" by him. . . If God is indeed giving himself, our task is to be in place to receive. The gaze of faith keeps us in that place.

- Iain Matthew

The more we pray, the more we please God, the more we obtain. I do not ask for those sweetnesses in prayer which God grants to certain souls. I am not worthy of them. I do not have enough strength to bear them. Extraordinary graces are not good for me. To give them to me would be to build upon the sand. It would be to pour a costly liqueur into a leaking cask which could hold nothing. I ask of God a prayer that is solid, simple, that will glorify him and not puff me up. Dryness and desolation, accompanied with God's grace, are very good for me I thi nk.

- *St. Claude de La Colombiere*

The best used hour in our lives is that in which we love Jesus the most. A soul does good, not in proportion to its knowledge or intellect, but to its holiness. I must embrace all men for God's sake in the same love and the same self- forgetfulness. I must be no more anxious about my own health and life than a tree is about a falling leaf. We must remember only Jesus, think only of Jesus, counting any loss as a profit insofar as it makes more room in us for thought about and knowledge of Jesus, beside whom everything else is nothing. *I must keep all my powers for God.*

- Blessed Charles de Foucauld

We have a double obligation which at first sight seems paradoxical, both to accept suffering and to wrestle with it. We are obliged to do all that we individually can to alleviate the pain and sickness of mind and body that afflicts mankind, to wage war on misery, want and injustice, to use every natural means given to us to do this . . . We as Christians live with Christ's life. He lives our life; we are offered the glory of living his. But on earth it is impossible to respond to this offer, which involves loving with his love, without accepting what he accepted as man. . . . The suffering of the whole world is the concern of each one of us.

- Caryll Houselander

What a sad thing it is to see that most people never even bother to think about the reason for their existence, but live as if they believe themselves created only to build houses, plant trees, cultivate the garden, pile up wealth, or do frivolous things. Consider your own past life. Say, "Lord, what was I thinking of when I was not thinking of you? Whom did I love when I was not loving you?"

- St. Francis de Sales

To say God is within us is to say that we are transcendent. . .He is our center, our term, our completion. . .We must be born again of the Spirit. Without the Spirit we remain flesh which cannot know God. The evolution of the butterfly is a marvelous image of what is meant here. The caterpillar must be "born again." It must receive an impetus to enable it to be transformed into a butterfly. But it has with it, in its caterpillar state, all the potential for this. Nothing new is added; what is already there is developed. So it is with us. God is our beloved in truth now, but will be so even more truly after long and generous effort and correspondence with his action. Then we are no longer our own, but his.

- Sister Ruth Burrows

J esus' response to our worry-filled lives . . . He asks us to shift the point of gravity, to relocate the center of our attention, to change our priorities. Jesus wants us to move from the "many things" to the "one necessary thing." . . . Jesus does not speak about a change of activities, a change in contacts, or even a change of pace. He speaks about a change of heart . . . What counts is where our hearts are. When we worry, we have our hearts in the wrong place. Jesus asks us to move our hearts to the center, where all other things fall into place. What is the center? Jesus calls it the kingdom, the kingdom of his Father.

- Henri Nouwen

Filling our minds with the memory of God and what he has done is one of the most important ways that we can experience his power to heal the hurts that reside in us, the ones we can't shake. Keeping God in our memory can help us to forgive what seems unforgivable. It helps us bring an end to the sins that nag at us, the ones we can't seem to control. It helps us when our burdens seem insurmountable. In all of these situations, God can use our memories to take us deeper into his heart, especially when we feel frustrated in our spiritual walk and distant from him. It's one of the major ways he renews our minds, and that is why it is so important that we remember him. Put the memory of God and his mighty deeds in the forefront of your minds - along with the place your loved ones hold. Better yet, put the memory of God above everyone and everything else.

- Anonymous

Give me Lord, a listening heart, a heart tuned into you, so that I do not miss your divine voice coming to me daily through others, in my personal hopes and fears, achievements and failures, joys and sorrows. Help me Jesus, to achieve a silent, receptive attitude, for it is only then that I will hear your voice calling me by name, and having attained this close relationship, there will no longer be any need for words.

- Sister Peter Dupree

We are to serve God. How we do this will depend on each one's personal vocation. God calls us to serve him in different ways . . . Christ lived the ordinary life of a carpenter of his day in Nazareth, and by doing so he has made holy all ordinary things and activities . . . Whatever we do looks different to the Father than it does to us. You have that floor to sweep. Nothing very dramatic in that. God sees more than the sweeping. He sees it as a service to him, and this is because his Son did that for thirty years of his life . . . Your daily work is your daily service to God. To make that service a loving one, adds to it, both in giving honor to God and in the joy you will experience.

- Cardinal Basil Hume

Jesus is the man who is the incarnation of the Truth. For this reason, before identifying himself as the Truth, Jesus calls himself the Way. Jesus is the Way to the Truth . . . We do not seek solutions to the problems of life derived from religious sentiments, spiritual approaches, or philosophical convictions . . . In each circumstance of life, whatever it is, we seek not an answer but a Presence . . . We do not come together as Church to find intellectual answers to our questions about the meaning and purpose of life. This is to reduce the Church to an ideology. We come together not to find answers but to learn how to recognize and affirm a Presence . . . We come together as the Church to learn how to recognize the fact of this Presence, and to witness to it in any circumstance of life, especially when there are no answers . . . Jesus Christ is the way to the answer.

- Monsignor Lorenzo Albacete

Christ comes to us full of perfect knowledge and unlimited love. He knows exactly what we are, and he knows exactly what our life will be . . . He knows all our mistakes and all our sins; he knows all our misfortunes and all our miseries. He knows all these things in advance, but being the perfect Lover, he comes with the power of God to heal all these ills. He is perfectly prepared to repair our life completely if we do not prevent him. And God is able to make all grace abound in you; that you always, having all sufficiency in all things, may abound to every good work. Our sufficiency is from God.

- Father Eugene Boylan, O.C.S.O.

To make possible true inner silence, practice: Silence of the eyes, by seeking always the beauty and goodness of God everywhere, closing them to the faults of others and to all that is sinful and disturbing to the soul. Silence of the ears, by listening always to the voice of God and to the cry of the poor and the needy, closing them to all other voices that come from fallen human nature, such as gossip, tale-bearing and uncharitable words. Silence of the tongue, by praising God . . . and by refraining from self-defense and every word that causes darkness, turmoil, pain, and death. Silence of the mind, by opening it to the truth and knowledge of God in prayer and contemplation . . . and by closing it to all untruths, distractions, destructive thoughts, rash judgments, false suspicions of others, vengeful thoughts, and desires. Silence of the heart, by loving God with our heart, soul, mind, and strength and one another as God loves, and avoiding all selfishness, hatred, envy, jealousy, and greed. I shall keep the silence of my heart with greater care, so that in the silence of my heart I hear His words of comfort . . . For in the silence and purity of the heart God speaks.

- Mother Teresa of Calcutta

We become transfigured by becoming little, humble, poor, dependent, powerless. How do we empty ourselves? How do we become little? By accepting all the sufferings that God permits to come into our lives. By seeking to serve others rather than to be served. By taking the last place. By never seeking recognition or applause. By making charity the foundation of our lives. By forgiving and loving our enemies.

- Father Frederick Miller

What we feel most of the time is our poverty without God. What we feel is our need for him, our, at times, pathetic lack of anything spiritually authentic or real in our life. It is into this darkness that God comes, all filled with light. It is into our poverty that he returns again and again without warning so that we might share with him the joy of rediscovered love . . . This is what our faith reveals to us - that even if we would go to the most distant, most unknown, most forsaken place, he would be there waiting for us. Even if our sins be as scarlet, we are to trust in him. Even if death itself overtakes us, *Nothing shall separate us from the love of God that comes to us in Christ Jesus our Lord* (Romans 8:38-39). Always he is with us and we in him, in an intimate communion beyond anything we can think or imagine.

- James Finley

Our life itself depends upon this living faith . . . That indeed, is what a Christian should be like, a person of quiet readiness and interior vigor. We should live deeply centered in the Holy Spirit . . . We should burn with a desire to save the people and not focus on our own little egos . . . On the one hand, Christian life is much simpler, but on the other hand, it is much more difficult, just because a great life must be taken seriously. The Christian must always view things from the great perspective of God and live accordingly . . . Our hearts must be keenly alert for opportunities in our own little corners of daily life. May we stand in this world, not as people in hiding, but as those who help prepare the way of the only begotten Son of God.

- Father Alfred Delp, S.J.

Grant me the grace today, Jesus, to accept your word and to place my trust in you as your Blessed Mother did. Let her be a model for me as a person who was willing to devote her whole life to serving your Father. She accepted your word and became your Mother. I am not faced with such an awesome responsibility, yet I often fail, and fail miserably, even in small things. I am weak; I am afraid. I often find it hard to believe . . . Lord, help me today to remember the example of your Mother, to know amid the confusion of everyday life that you are truly with me, that your kingdom is at hand.

- Robert Meehan

Yu who are beyond time, Lord, you know what you are doing. You make no mistakes in your distribution of time to men. . .But we must not lose time, waste time, or kill time, for time is a gift that you give us . . . The time that you give me, the years of my life, the days of my years, the hours of my days, they are mine to fill and to offer to you. I am not asking you Lord for time to do this and then that, but your grace to do conscientiously, in the time that you have given me, what you want me to do.

- Father Michel Quoist

Dear Lord, help me to keep my eyes on you. You are the incarnation of Divine Love, you are the expression of God's infinite compassion, you are the visible manifestation of the Father's holiness. You are beauty, goodness, gentleness, forgiveness, and mercy. In you all can be found. Outside of you, nothing can be found. Why should I look elsewhere or go elsewhere? You have the words of eternal life . . . You are the light that shines in the darkness . . . You are the perfect icon of God. In and through you I can see and find my way to the Heavenly Father.

- Henri Nouwen

Many of our problems derive from the fact that we do not trust God; that we allow ourselves to be thrown back on self, to depend on self, to look for our salvation within our own resources - our thinking, ability, talents . . . We must live in the present with the task which is ours today, with the people with whom our lot is cast. We must live in this world renewed and refashioned by Christ by reason of the Incarnation. We must look forward to the future, when all will be peace, serenity, happiness. Perhaps in our contemporary spirituality we think too little of the joy of heaven, the happiness of heaven. It is good to look forward with expectation, with excitement, to the moment when we shall . . . be with Christ, be with Christ in the Father. This is the kind of grace for which we ought to be praying, the expectation with which we should look forward, thus putting into perspective - God's perspective - the things of the world: our problems, our desires, our lives.

- Cardinal Basil Hume

Jesus was born far away from his own country at a severe season of the year and in extreme poverty. Shortly afterwards, behold him persecuted by Herod. He takes flight, and while in exile suffers from the hardships he had to bear, and with those of the Blessed Virgin and St. Joseph, who had to endure much for his sake. When he returned to Nazareth and grew up, he submitted himself to his parents and to the rules of a hidden life, so as to serve as a model for religious souls . . . And it is without a doubt that he was thinking of you then, and had you in view, in the eternal design he had of saving you . . . You will see how he suffered, how he prayed, how he labored and how he obeyed.

- St. Vincent de Paul

St. Paul had a great and broad vision; he saw God's plan from its beginning to its fulfillment. In one of his resounding sentences he wrote, *But when the time had fully come, God sent forth his Son, born of a woman, born under the law.* In the same vein, Paul assures us that Christ died at the appointed time. What do we mean by appointed time? . . . Only the Lord of history, who sees all of history at once, could fix the appointed time. This truth of our faith should be deeply consoling. We are not adrift on a boundless sea of yesterdays and tomorrows; God has fitted us into his great plan . . . If Christ is the beginning and the end, then he embraces us and our lives, and our short days are taken up into his endless time.

- Father Joseph T. Lienhard, S.J.

Twelve stars for reaching the highest perfection: love of God, love of neighbor, obedience, chastity, poverty, attendance at choir, penance, humility, mortification, prayer, silence, peace.

- St. John of the Cross

Do you know what it is to have a friend in a distant country, to expect news of him, and to wonder from day to day what he is now doing, and whether he is well? Do you know what it is to have a person present with you, that your eyes follow his, that you anticipate his wishes, that you smile in his smile, are sad in his sadness, are downcast when he is vexed, and rejoice in his successes? To watch for Christ is a feeling such as these, as far as feelings of this world are fit to shadow those of another. He watches for Christ who has a sensitive, eager mind; who is awake, alive, quick-sighted and zealous in seeking and honoring him; who looks for him in all that happens, and who would not be surprised . . . or overwhelmed, if he found that he was coming at once.

- Blessed John Henry Newman

Our life is a sacramental life . . . It is more in frailty than in strength that Christ reveals himself upon earth; more in littleness than in greatness; more in lowliness than in glory; for he is the Way and such is the Way of Love. Christ said, *It is expedient to you that I go.* It is expedient, indeed. For nothing else but his going breaks the hard crust of our complacency and forces us to go out from ourselves to seek him.

- Caryll Houselander

Mary was so very much like the rest of us in so many ways. Her parents were responsible for her coming into the world, just like yours and mine. Her life, both before and after her marriage to St. Joseph, was exactly like the one that thousands of women living today are leading - from all outward appearances. I must remind myself frequently Lord, that you want me to be a saint. The task is not an easy one but the opportunity is there. You have given me the very same opportunities to love you, as you gave to your Mother. Help me to remember to use her life as my model. Each day, in my very ordinary existence, you send me crosses to offer up and joys to thank you for. Help me to recognize them as Mary did.

- Father John Maguire

Humility is attractive to God. Everywhere that it is found, there God is. And everywhere that God is here below, he clothes himself, as it were, with a garment that conceals his presence from the proud and reveals it to the simple and the little ones. When Jesus came to this world, it was as an infant wrapped in swaddling clothes. That was the sign given to the shepherds: *And this shall be a sign to you,* the angel said. *You will find an infant wrapped in swaddling clothes and lying in a manger.* The sign of humility always marks the Divine here below.

- P. Marie-Eugene, O.C.D.

My dear friend, in the body I am at Nazareth but in spirit I have been at Bethlehem for the last month. As I write to you I feel as though I am with Mary and Joseph beside the Crib. It is good to be there. Outside are the cold and the snow, images of the world, but in the little cave, lit by the light of Jesus, it is sweet and warm and light. Father Abbot asks me what it is the Divine Child whispers to me all this month as I watch at his feet at night between his holy parents, when he comes into my arms and enters into my heart in Holy Communion. He says over and over again, "The will of God, the will of God. Behold I come." In the beginning of the book of life it is written that I should do thy will. The will of God and the will of God through obedience, this is what the beloved voice of the Divine Child gently murmurs to me.

- Blessed Charles de Foucauld

I ask the Most High, "Where do you dwell?" He answers, "Each day I have a new dwelling, a new birth, in a cave, in a lowly abode. I am happy in a lowly soul, in a crib." I still keep asking Jesus where he dwells. "In a cave," he answers. "Do you know how I have crushed the enemy? By being born so low."

- Blessed Mary of Jesus Crucified

Most of us in the world today live far from Jesus Christ, the incarnate God who came to dwell amongst us. We live our lives by philosophies amid worldly affairs and occupations that totally absorb us and are a great distance from the manger. In all kinds of ways, God has to prod us and reach out to us again and again so that we can manage to escape from the muddle of our thoughts and activities and discover the way that leads to him. But a path exists for all of us. The Lord provides everyone with tailor-made signals. He calls each one of us so that we too can say, "Come on, let us go over to Bethlehem – to the God who has come to meet us." Yes, indeed. God has set out towards us. Left to ourselves we could not reach him. The path is too much for our strength. But God has come down. He comes towards us. He has traveled the longer part of the journey. Now he invites us: "Come and see how much I love you. Come and see that I am here."

- Pope Benedict XVI

December 23

J ust as nature retreats deep into itself during the winter months, so the Christian is invited to turn inward during the blessed time of Advent in preparation for the Lord's coming . . . Advent is a quiet contemplative time of waiting for the Light that will come and shine on us on Christmas Day, rescuing us from the great darkness and hopelessness we experience in our daily lives.

- Brother Victor-Antoine D'Avila-Latourrette

Christ rested in Mary - still, silent, helpless, utterly dependent. The Creator trusted himself to his creature . . . His hands were folded; her hands did the work of his hands. His life was her life; his heartbeat was the beating of her heart. This was a foreshadowing of what the Incarnation would mean for us; for in us, too, Christ rests as he rested in Mary. From the moment when the Christ-life is conceived in us, our life is intended for one thing, the expression of his love, his love for God and for the world. Our words are to be the words he wants us to speak; we must go to wherever he wants to go, we must see and look at whatever he wants to see and look at; the work that our hands do must be the work that his hands want to do; our life must be the living of his life, our loves, the loving of his heart.

- Caryll Houselander

Our Lord asks us to let the life continue in us that he began on earth in the womb of the Virgin Mary. Let him live in us; let his hidden life in Nazareth continue in us; let his life of universal charity continue in us; let his life of humility be prolonged in us. Let Jesus continue to light a fire on the earth by making each moment of our lives become moments of his life - all our thoughts, our words, and actions become thoughts and words and actions that are no longer natural or human but Divine, no longer our own but those of Jesus.

- Blessed Charles de Foucauld

It is no use saying that we are born two thousand years too late to give room to Christ. Nor will those who live at the end of the world have been born too late. Christ is always with us, always asking for room in our heart. But now it is with the voice of our contemporaries that he speaks, with the eyes of store clerks, factory workers, and children that he gazes; with the hands of office workers, slum dwellers, and suburban housewives that he gives. It is with the feet of soldiers and tramps that he walks, and with the heart of anyone in need that he longs for shelter. And giving shelter or food to anyone who asks for it, or needs it, is giving it to Christ.

- Dorothy Day

We are not giving ourselves only to an idea, however great; we are not giving ourselves only to the pursuit of a perfection, however true. We are giving ourselves to a Person, a living person who is God, and God who is our brother . . . because he is also a man. Our deepest aim is to live a real and total friendship with Jesus, in the midst of the world. It is for the sake of him, that we work and struggle. It is in order to meet the call of his love upon us that we are so often on our knees, at his feet, trying to learn to love him - to love him as our God, to love him as our Friend, to love him as our Brother. First and last, our effort of faith will be in the direction of a personal meeting, for we are certain that we cannot lose our way if we cling to the Lord with our whole being, if we place our lives in his hands - in the hands of him who is the Way itself, the Truth itself, the Life itself.

- Father Rene Voillaume

In life and in death, keep close to Jesus and give yourself into his faithful keeping; he alone can help you when all others fail you. He is of such a kind, this beloved friend of yours, that he will not share your love with another; he wishes to have your heart for himself alone, to reign there like a king seated on his rightful throne. If only you knew the way to empty your heart of all things created. If you did, how gladly would Jesus come and make his home with you. When you put your trust in men, excluding Jesus, you will find that it is nearly all a complete loss.

- Thomas à Kempis

Jesus Christ is the same yesterday, today and forever. He waits for you in the ciborium, your Friend of yesterday; the Friend whose intimacy you have so often forgotten, and more than once have even betrayed. All that he has forgiven you, as a friend does . . . Your Friend yesterday - Your Friend today, when you are so little conscious of the need for such a friendship . . . His Love, so little felt and so little realized, is strengthening itself in your heart, waiting for the day when you will need it more. Your Friend today, your Friend forever . . . His friendship will remain unaltered; His Presence in the Blessed Sacrament will still wait for you, the same as ever . . . And at last when death comes, all earthly ties must slip away from you, even then this Friendship will be yours . . . Your Friend forever.

- Monsignor Ronald Knox

Christ came, and comes now, so that we should have life and have it in its fullness . . . He is the Father and Mother whose heart never sleeps, whose hands never lift from their works that they have made. He is the one who has numbered the hairs on our heads. In his humanity, we are clothed as in a warm woolen garment. In him we live as in our home. He is our food and our drink, our shade in the heat, our comfort in sorrow, our healing when we are wounded, our light in darkness.

- Caryll Houselander

The last day of a year of which the chief characteristic for me has been privation. God willed it to be full enough of suffering, renunciation, sadness of every kind . . . But the blessed Master taught me stronger, deeper love, stripped of conscious happiness; and it is from the bottom of my heart that I offer him the year that is gone, and the one that is to come. I consecrate myself to him and accept all that he wants of me, through me, or for me; joy or sorrow, health or illness, poverty or riches, and also life or death . . . For myself, I ask one thing: let me love thee, without joy or comfort if need be, and use me for the spreading of thy spiritual kingdom in souls, Jesus my Savior.

- Elisabeth Leseur

Made in the USA
Lexington, KY
28 September 2012